Church Councils

100 QUESTIONS AND ANSWERS

PAUL SENZ

Church Councils

100 QUESTIONS AND ANSWERS

IGNATIUS PRESS   SAN FRANCISCO

Cover photo:
Between sessions at the Second Vatican Council
© Giancarlo Giuliani/Catholicpressphoto

Cover design by Enrique J. Aguilar

© 2023 by Ignatius Press, San Francisco
All rights reserved
ISBN 978-1-62164-511-5 (PB)
ISBN 978-1-64229-253-4 (eBook)
Library of Congress Control Number 2022946630
Printed in the United States of America ∞

To Dr. Michael Cameron, Fr. Charles Connor, and Joseph Cardinal Ratzinger, who taught me to love and cherish the history of the Catholic Church

CONTENTS

FOREWORD

by Mike Aquilina

I grew up at a time when there was only one council. When my religion teachers spoke of "The Council", they were not talking about Nicaea or Ephesus or Fourth Lateran or Trent. They were speaking in a tense that still seemed present. The Second Vatican Council had closed in 1965, but in 1980 it was as if the conciliar bishops' after-shave still lingered in the air.

Vatican II dominated the news while it was in session, and it remained a hot topic for decades afterward. Decades passed, and I entered middle age, and priests at the pulpit still spoke of "The Council", and so did lecturers at Catholic events. Everyone understood, because The Council was still a matter of seismic effect for us. It had significantly changed the liturgy—the most visible and common element of Catholic identity. Everybody alive felt the change. And we experienced it anew at irregular intervals as the ritual tweaks continued, always explained as attempts to be more faithful to The Council.

We spoke of Vatican II as if it were a singularity in Church history.

It was not, of course. My great-grandparents had been alive to witness the drama of The Council's predecessor. The First Vatican Council shocked the world with its definition of papal infallibility. Then the bishops dispersed dramatically, without adjournment, as troops from the newly founded Kingdom of Italy seized Rome and drove Pope Pius IX to withdraw into the Vatican as a "prisoner".

So, no matter what we were thinking in the 1960s, our council was neither unique nor even exceptional. It was indeed a big deal, but it was a big deal because it was a council—a general or ecumenical council—and those are always a big deal.

Only twenty-one are recognized by the Catholic Church, and sometimes entire centuries go by without one happening. Indeed, ninety-two years passed between the abrupt suspension of Vatican I and the much-hyped opening of Vatican II.

Each council represents a moment of "The Church in Crisis", to steal a defining phrase from the historian Philip Hughes. When scholars set out to write histories of the Catholic Church, the general councils often represent an important structural element in the books. The councils have all the stuff necessary to carry a narrative forward: conflict, high drama, important personages, heroes and villains, passionate speeches that spell out arguments in detail. Historians want their histories to be read, and crises make for stories that engage readers.

When we think about the councils today, we do so in terms of an elaborately developed theology. We have full awareness of the trials and errors of centuries of bishops' meetings. We know about the edges beyond which there are dragons and the error of conciliarism. But it is good for us to recall that the fathers of the early councils had no such resources. Those who attended the first general council, at Nicaea in A.D. 325, knew that their meeting was important because the emperor was there for it —and the food was superlative. But they did not know they were introducing a new mode by which the Church would ever afterward exercise her authority. They were, in a sense, trapped in their historical moment as my contemporaries and I were trapped in the 1960s. We could not see the forest of councils because of the one tree we were hugging (or kicking) with all our might.

God bless Paul Senz, because he has given us a way to transcend our historical moment and appreciate all the general councils, and councils in general. He has given us the definitions we need if we would advance in understanding. He answers the questions that arise quite naturally when we are reading those great histories of the Church.

He has done all of this well, and none of this is easily done, because the history of the councils is still history in the making. Though we may know more about the subject than the fathers did when they arrived at Nicaea, we know far less than our far descendants will know as they tune in to the news of the most recent of the councils—though surely they will know its special import no more than the fathers in 325 knew Nicaea's.

Perhaps this book will survive at least to raise the question—and answer so many others.

BRIEF PREFATORY NOTE

When it comes down to it, this is a book about the teaching authority of the Catholic Church and the different ways in which that authority is exercised—with a focus on one particular expression of that authority, the ecumenical council.

The history of the councils gives a pretty fair summary of the history of the Catholic Church. A survey of this history will expose one to most of the important teachings, events, figures, and movements that have impacted the Church through the centuries. And a deep understanding of the theology behind ecumenical councils also helps one to understand the Church's hierarchy and even why Christ founded the Church with Peter and a college of apostles.

This book is about much more than the history of the councils, although that history will be covered. It is about the teaching authority of the Church and the protection of the Holy Spirit. It is about how the apostles and their successors, the bishops, have worked through millennia to keep the Barque of Peter from capsizing and to fulfill Our Lord's command that they go out and teach all nations.

I hope this book will answer some basic questions for the reader and serve as inspiration to dive more deeply into the history of the councils and into Church history more broadly. This is a basic survey of that history, and there are many resources available out there for a deeper dive—first and foremost, the documents of the councils themselves.

ACKNOWLEDGMENTS

This book is not merely the fruit of my own labors. I am indebted to numerous people for their assistance, guidance, and prayers—and to many others for their work, which served as incredibly helpful resources.

The most important resource I had at my fingertips was the phenomenal book *Teaching with Authority* by Jimmy Akin, published by Catholic Answers Press. Mr. Akin's gift for succinctly and clearly elucidating the material made this book a tremendously helpful resource.

Such eminent Church historians as Mike Aquilina, Steve Weidenkopf, and James Papandrea were kind enough (and patient enough) to answer many questions, point me in the direction of other sources, and help me see the broader picture. I am grateful for their attentiveness and encouragement.

And thank God for my many heavenly intercessors and friends, this great cloud of witnesses.

Last, but certainly not least, I must acknowledge my wife, Chantel, and our (now five—welcome to the world, Josephine!) wonderful children, who both encouraged me to continue writing and coaxed me *away* from the desk once in a while. I would accomplish nothing without their prayers and support.

GENERAL QUESTIONS

1. What is a council?

The *Catholic Encyclopedia* defines councils as "legally convened assemblies of ecclesiastical dignitaries and theological experts for the purpose of discussing and regulating
matters of church doctrine and discipline." This is a broad
definition, as there are many different types of councils
that could fall under that term. When people talk about
Church councils, what they typically are talking about—
and what this book mostly addresses—are the *ecumenical
councils*.

We first find the term "ecumenical council" used by
the great Church historian Eusebius of Caesarea (d. ca.
A.D. 340). He uses the term to describe the Council of
Nicaea in his book on the life of the Roman emperor
Constantine (d. A.D. 337).

The 1983 *Code of Canon Law* (*Codex Iuris Canonici*, or
CIC) updated the Church's legislation and regulations on
ecumenical councils and the way the college of bishops
functions in that context. Among other things, it emphasized that the pope retains his primacy and that an ecumenical council is not superior to the pope. In fact, the
Code of Canon Law penalizes those who appeal to an ecumenical council or the college of bishops as a whole over
and against the pope (can. 1372).

As we will see throughout this book, this has been debated many times in the history of the Church. But the pope retains supreme authority over ecumenical councils and in fact is the sole arbiter of whether or not a council is ecumenical.

At an ecumenical council, the bishops of the world gather to discuss matters crucial to the life of the Church, and the council produces some documents or takes some actions intended to support the Church.

The fact that an ecumenical council is, by definition, a gathering of the world's bishops ratified by the pope is what gives the gathering its authority. Saint Athanasius, for example, argued that the Council of Nicaea was particularly sacred because bishops from all parts of the world were in attendance. (He would have been astounded to see the wide array of bishops present at the Second Vatican Council!)

2. How often do councils happen?

Councils are not held at regular intervals; a council is called by the competent authority (the pope, in the case of an ecumenical council) when he discerns a particular need for all the bishops of the world to come together to address a matter of special importance for the Church. In some cases, there are only a few decades between ecumenical councils; in other cases it has been a few centuries.

The shortest interval between councils was sixteen years (between the First and Second Lateran Councils in the twelfth century [or thirteen years, if you consider the *end* of the Council of Constance and the *beginning* of the Council of Basel/Ferrara/Florence]), and the longest was 324 years (between the beginnings of the Council of Trent and the First Vatican Council).

3. What prompts a council to be called, then?

Councils are always called in response to a particular need. Nowadays, when some problem or question arises that the pope feels or agrees needs to be addressed by the bishops of the world all teaching in unison, he convenes an ecumenical council so that the matter may be discussed and discerned and so that the bishops can officially teach from a united front. As we will see in later questions, sometimes it is a need to refute a certain heresy that has crept in, while at other times a council is called due to some wide pastoral need in the Church. Other pastoral or teaching gatherings of bishops—such as synods, regional councils, meetings of national bishops conferences—may be called for other reasons or may even occur at regular intervals.

4. Who participates in a council?

This has varied somewhat over the centuries, but there are typically a few different participants in a council: the council fathers (bishops in attendance); whatever assistants or secretaries are brought by the bishops; theological advisers; and observers invited by the pope or the bishops.

As for the default, official "guest list" of an ecumenical

council, we find a clear description of this in the *Code of Canons of the Eastern Churches*: "It is the right and obligation of all and only the bishops who are members of the college of bishops to participate in an ecumenical council with a deliberative vote" (*Codex Canonum Ecclesiarum Orientalium*, or *CCEO* 52, par. 1). So the bishops of the world—the "college of bishops", meaning those bishops who are validly *and* licitly ordained and who are in communion with the Holy Father—not only have a right to participate in an ecumenical council, they have an obligation to do so. This is an important part of their teaching office as successors to the apostles, to teach in union with each other, and participating in an ecumenical council is the clearest and most fundamental way of doing so.

There are others who may be invited or called to participate, apart from the bishops who are obligated to do so: "The supreme authority of the Church can also call others who are not bishops to an ecumenical council and determine what part they take in it" (*CCEO* 52, par. 2).

5. What is a "council father"?

The bishops in attendance are called "council fathers". In some cases, there were people other than just the bishops who played significant roles in the day-to-day proceedings of the council—and Protestants and Orthodox have been invited to the more recent councils (Trent, Vatican I, and Vatican II, but only as observers). But the "council fathers", who are truly responsible for the council's basic operations and who have the authority collegially to decide on the questions at hand, are the bishops in union with the pope.

6. Why are only these men council fathers?

The authority of the council derives from the fact that the bishops of the world are the successors of the apostles, and when teaching together they are fulfilling Christ's command that they teach all nations. This is why the bishops, quite apart from any others who may be in attendance or participating in the council in other ways, are considered the "fathers" of the council.

As is often the case in regard to councils, it comes down to a question of authority. While all Christians are called to preach the gospel (cf. Mt 28:19–20) and teach the truth to others, this is a particular calling of the clergy, and especially of bishops. In the Prophet Malachi, we read: "For the lips of a priest should guard knowledge, and men should seek instruction from his mouth, for he is the messenger of the LORD of hosts" (Mal 2:7). In the First Letter to Timothy, Saint Paul tells us that a bishop should be an "apt teacher" (1 Tim 3:2), and "Let the elders who rule well be considered worthy of double honor, especially those who labor in preaching and teaching" (1 Tim 5:17). After all, bishops are the successors of the apostles, and the teaching office, the power to bind and loose (cf. Mt 18:18), and the special responsibility for safeguarding the deposit of faith and governing the Church (cf. 1 Tim 6:20 and 2 Tim 1:14; Acts 20:28) are communicated to them through ordination.

7. Are there others who participate in a council, apart from the "fathers"?

Yes, there are many people involved in a council, with very different responsibilities. Most of these are involved for practical and logistical reasons—such as secretaries, assistants, organizers, not to mention security, hospitality, etc.—but do not have any role of authority in the proceedings. In addition to these individuals, however, there are those who are more directly involved in the council proceedings, but without authority or voting power, such as theological advisers or non-Catholic "observers".

8. Are there different types of councils?

Yes, there are many different types of councils that can be seen in the Church's history. The differences essentially boil down to how wide a swath of the Church was represented and the authority of the bishops participating. For example, the Council of Constantinople (381) —now recognized as the second ecumenical council— was initially a general synod of the East, with only the Eastern patriarchs and bishops in attendance, but it later gained the rank of an ecumenical council when the pope accepted and ratified the council's decrees for application in the worldwide Church.

The current *Code of Canon Law* still makes provision for three official types of councils: Diocesan Synods, which typically involve only one bishop (although if the diocese has auxiliary bishops or a coadjutor bishop, they may also be involved) and is only addressing the diocesan territory (cf. *CIC* 460–68); particular councils, which can be either plenary (complete) or provincial, depending on whether they involve all the bishops in a national episcopal conference or only those in a given region (cf. *CIC* 439–46); and ecumenical councils (cf. *CIC* 337–41).

The different types of councils, and the different level and breadth of authority each holds, ultimately come down to the number of bishops involved and the intention of the gathering. A national conference of bishops cannot make decisions for the universal Church, for example; and a synod of bishops that meets to advise the pope cannot make an infallible decree on some doctrinal matter. But because ecumenical councils bring together all the bishops of the world, in union with the pope, and they intend to teach authoritatively the whole Church, they have universal authority.

9. What does "ecumenical" mean?

The term "ecumenical" comes from the Greek *oikoumene*, which means "the whole inhabited world". In ecclesiastical contexts, it refers to the entire universal Church—for example, *ecumenism* is the term for efforts toward Christian unity—the unity of *all* who profess faith in Christ. You may hear about "ecumenical dialogue" when the pope meets with the Patriarch of Constantinople or when theologian representatives from Protestant and Catholic traditions gather to discuss or to draft a joint declaration on some theological point or another.

In the context of Church councils, "ecumenical" means that bishops from the whole Catholic Church all over the world are in attendance, and the council fathers are engaging in work that will affect the entire worldwide Church.

10. What makes a council "ecumenical"?

In order to be considered ecumenical, a council nowadays must be called by the pope (*CIC* 338), and the bishops of the whole world must teach in union with the pope. In practice, this means that the pope calls the council, presides over it, and makes the final decision and ratification of the council's decrees. Because the ecumenical council is the fullest expression of the teaching authority of the bishops, as the successors of the apostles, in union with the Holy Father, as the successor of Peter, the Church recognizes in such a gathering the supreme authority and power in the universal Church (cf. *CCC* 891). Historically, there have been many councils that were not convened or presided over by the pope, but only those that were accepted and ratified by the pope are now considered ecumenical.

11. How many ecumenical councils have there been?

As of the writing of this book, the Catholic Church recognizes twenty-one ecumenical councils. As we will see, different ecclesial groups outside full communion with the Catholic Church have different criteria for a council to be ecumenical, and even different criteria for whether or not they accept a council's teachings. The Eastern Orthodox churches, various Protestant denominations, and others recognize only certain councils as ecumenical. But the

Catholic Church—which is to say, the Church that has the *authority* to declare a council ecumenical—recognizes twenty-one thus far.

12. What are they, and when did they take place?

First Council of Nicaea (A.D. 325)
First Council of Constantinople (A.D. 381)
Council of Ephesus (A.D. 431)
Council of Chalcedon (A.D. 451)
Second Council of Constantinople (A.D. 553)
Third Council of Constantinople (A.D. 680–681)
Second Council of Nicaea (A.D. 787)
Fourth Council of Constantinople (A.D. 869)
First Council of the Lateran (A.D. 1123)
Second Council of the Lateran (A.D. 1139)
Third Council of the Lateran (A.D. 1179)
Fourth Council of the Lateran (A.D. 1215)
First Council of Lyons (A.D. 1245)
Second Council of Lyons (A.D. 1274)
Council of Vienne (A.D. 1311–1313)
Council of Constance (A.D. 1414–1418)
Council of Basel/Ferrara/Florence (A.D. 1431–1449)
Fifth Council of the Lateran (A.D. 1512–1517)
Council of Trent (A.D. 1545–1563)
First Vatican Council (A.D. 1869–1870)
Second Vatican Council (A.D. 1962–1965)

Later in this book, we will take a look at the context of each council, what prompted its calling, and what ultimately happened as a result.

13. Do all Christians agree on this?

All Christians certainly agree that each of these gatherings *happened*, but they do not all agree that all of these
councils had any authority or can be considered "ecumenical".

The recognition of a council as ecumenical has not always been as cut-and-dried a process as it is now. When
the Second Vatican Council was called in the twentieth
century, there was no question that it was an ecumenical
council. Pope Pius XII had considered calling a new ecumenical council during his pontificate, and his successor,
Pope Saint John XXIII, soon called one of his own. However, in the past this has not always been the case with
other councils—there have been some that were not initially considered ecumenical and only later attained that
designation.

Of the councils recognized by the Catholic Church as
ecumenical, the Orthodox recognize the first seven, and
Protestants typically the first seven or even just the first
four, depending on their own traditions and theological
lineage.

The Protestant recognition of ecumenical councils is a
complex web to unravel: not only is there a great deal of
variety in the Protestant acceptance of councils, but even
for those they accept, their understanding of the role and
function of a council is very different from that of the
Catholic and Orthodox. We do not have sufficient space
in this book to delve into the matter too deeply, but suf-
fice it to say that Protestants' understanding of ecclesiol-
ogy, the nature of what the Church *is*, and the teaching

authority of the Church's members (and clergy in particular) plays a significant role in their refusal to acknowledge the later Church councils. (Of course, their decision to accept the decrees of the *early* councils is inconsistent with this . . . but again, the scope of the present book is not sufficient for exploring this problem.)

14. How do they decide the location of a council?

There are many factors that go into deciding the location of a council, and each council has had its reasons for being held where it was held. Sometimes the location was decided for political reasons, sometimes logistical reasons. For example, the Council of Trent was held in that city because its location would allow relatively easy access to the council for Protestants in Germany and elsewhere in Europe (although no Protestants attended).

With the relatively recent availability of air travel, which allows thousands of bishops from all over the world to participate in a council, one of the chief considerations for location is the practicality of hosting. The logistics of housing and feeding all those bishops, theologians, advisors, etc., not to mention the press conferences, the smaller meetings of bishops, the large communal Masses —all of this makes for a logistical nightmare. But for many reasons, the Vatican is already set up to handle just such an eventuality. In light of all this, it seems highly likely that any future ecumenical council will once again be held at the Vatican. But such a decision would be up to the pope who calls the council—presumably based on a great deal of advice.

15. I've heard of synods of bishops; how are these not a council? What's the difference?

The main thing that distinguishes a synod of bishops from an ecumenical council is the intention for, and scope of, the gathering: the synod of bishops is meant to advise the pope and, thus, does not have any doctrinal authority in and of itself. Synods of bishops also are not intended to be gatherings of all the bishops of the world in union with the pope. Rather, think of them more as representatives from various regions, theological experts, and more coming together to discuss a topic on which the Holy Father would like the Church to reflect and on which he may like some advice.

This can be confusing, as at times in the Church's history the terms "council" and "synod" have been treated as synonyms. (It doesn't help that ecumenical councils are also sometimes called "universal" or "general" councils —both of which terms have also been used to refer to smaller councils, so long as they are larger than a single province.)

The meetings of the synods of bishops are meant to "foster closer unity between the Roman pontiff and the bishops" (*CIC* 342) and to advise the pope on the matter brought to bear in the synod's proceedings. Bishops and others are called from all over the world, meant to represent a wide swath of the Church and to deliberate and advise the pope. Usually, following these synods ("ordinary" synods occur at regular intervals, "extraordinary" synods can be called by the pope at any time), the Holy

Father will write and issue a post-synodal apostolic exhortation, a document that summarizes the deliberations and counsel of the synod and teaches the Church—usually on pastoral matters.

16. Do the councils change Church teaching?

The Church was founded by Christ to proclaim, preserve, and protect the truth in the deposit of faith, not to change existing teaching or create new beliefs out of whole cloth. Public revelation ended with the death of the last apostle (*CCC* 66)—God is no longer revealing new information to the Church. Sacred Scripture and Tradition contain the deposit of faith that is safeguarded by the Church. But Church councils, as with the Church's ordinary magisterium, can newly elaborate teachings or even solemnly define something that has long been believed or understood but never officially detailed.

When we look at the history of the councils, we will see many examples of teachings being discerned and solemnly defined in response to some prominent heresy. The most obvious example is the way in which the Church's understanding of the person of Jesus Christ, the Holy Spirit, and the Trinity were discerned and worked out over the course of many centuries and in half a dozen ecumenical councils. The Church's understanding of the truth can and does develop over time, but no ecumenical council can or will *create* new teachings or *fundamentally change* Church teaching. When it is a question of pastoral practice or discipline, that is another story.

*17. What does a council look like, practically
speaking? On a day to day basis, what happens?*

The daily rhythms of an ecumenical council revolve around prayer, particularly the Holy Sacrifice of the Mass and the Divine Office. With these at the heart of the council's proceedings, the council fathers engage in theological reflections, discussions, debates, and committee meetings.

*18. Has this changed over the centuries, or did it
always look like this?*

This has certainly changed somewhat over the centuries, and from council to council. Even just considering the logistical issues that differ in different locations and with different numbers of bishops in attendance, the day-to-day workings of a council will be different. At the First Council of Constantinople, for example, there were only about 150 bishops in attendance, whereas the Second Vatican Council saw more than 2,000 bishops descend on Rome, making for a complicated logistical situation. Even coordinating Masses with so many bishops would prove to be a logistical nightmare, let alone housing, feeding, and shuttling them around. When you add to the mix the fact that they come from many different language groups as well, things get even more complicated.

But the frame of the council's daily activity remains the same: prayer, discussion, and study. This approach was essentially established at the so-called Council of Jerusalem (cf. Acts 15).

19. Since bishops come from all over the world, how do they communicate at a council?

At the early Church councils, the Fathers may have spoken Latin or Greek, depending on which part of the empire they were coming from. And as we have seen, many of the councils were even held in the eastern part of the empire, so Greek may well have been the *lingua franca* of those councils. For the most part, council business and interactions between bishops were conducted in Latin or Italian. For various reasons (including the fact that many of them did theological studies in Rome at some point), many of the world's bishops can speak Italian. However, Latin remains the official language of the Church, and prior to the Second Vatican Council it was standard for priests (and thus, of course, bishops) to be proficient in Latin. As this was the first ecumenical council that was attended by a truly worldwide episcopacy, having a single universal ecclesiastical language came in quite handy, allowing bishops and theologians from widely diverse cultures and mother tongues to communicate with each other with ease.

More than likely, any council held in the near future would feature a melting pot of languages. Bishops no longer are fluent in Latin, and there is no single language they all could converse in. Certain official aspects of the council would likely be in Latin, while the day-to-day operations would be in Italian, and the bishops would be divided up by language group for committees and discussions. Additionally, real-time translations are routinely used at meetings of the Synod of Bishops, as is done at the United Nations. Something similar would likely happen at future ecumenical councils.

20. Who calls a council?

While this has varied somewhat over the centuries, now it is clearly stated in the *Code of Canon Law* that only the pope can call a council. "It is for the Roman Pontiff alone to convoke an ecumenical council, to preside over it personally or through others, to transfer, suspend or dissolve it, and to approve its decrees" (*CIC*, can. 338, par. 1).

21. Who decides what is to be discussed at a council, and how is this decided?

Once again, this is the purview and responsibility of the pope. Of course, in practice, the pope does not make such decisions unilaterally; typically, this is the result of much consultation with bishops, priests, theologians, professors, men and women religious, and lay people all around the world. But ultimately, the decision is the Holy Father's. This is detailed in the *Code of Canon Law*: "It is for the same Roman Pontiff to determine matters to be treated in a council and to establish the order to be followed in a council; to the questions proposed by the Roman Pontiff the fathers of a council can add other questions, to be approved by the same Roman Pontiff" (can. 338, par. 2).

22. The emperor used to convene them—when did it start being only the pope?

We should keep in mind that the emperors did not convene "ecumenical councils" as such. For example, Constantine convened the First Council of Nicaea, which is considered the first ecumenical council. Emperors convened councils, gatherings of bishops from around the region or around the empire, to deliberate and resolve theological issues of the day. But the way we understand ecumenical councils today is not how Constantine and the other emperors would have understood them. A council does not become ecumenical unless and until it is recognized as such by the pope. In fact, as we have seen, at least one council (the First Council of Constantinople in A.D. 381) was initially merely a synod of the East, until the pope ratified its decrees for the universal Church, making it an ecumenical council.

The relationship between Church and State under the Roman Empire was complicated. Once Christianity was no longer illegal, and even more so once it was the official religion of the empire, the emperors played pivotal roles in the affairs of the Church. This led at times to great conflicts between emperors and popes, and many emperors understood themselves to be responsible for ensuring the integrity of the faith. (This does not mean they were all unflinchingly orthodox; in fact, many of them were downright heretics.) Just as Constantine had done at Nicaea, emperors had the authority to call councils, even though the theological and doctrinal authority remained in the hands of the bishops.

Pope Gregory VII, who reigned from A.D. 1073 to 1085, explicitly claimed for himself the authority to summon councils (as well as other papal prerogatives such as appointing bishops, canonizing saints, and more). He claimed this authority based on the power to bind and loose that Jesus gave to the apostles, and also to Peter in particular (and, thus, to their successors).

Today, since there is not the same political machination and involvement as in the time of the Roman Empire, the pope can convene an ecumenical council. The Second Vatican Council was convened explicitly as the twenty-first ecumenical council in the Church's history; it was called by the Holy Father, with the intention from the beginning that it be ecumenical.

23. When the emperor called the council, did he get to make the final call on the council's decisions?

It would be fair to say that, at times, the emperors thought they had ultimate power and authority over ecclesiastical matters, including questions of doctrine and discipline, because of the sway they held over bishops. But they were mistaken. Even if the emperor convoked a council, and even if he shepherded the council through its daily proceedings, and even if he exerted influence (sometimes through threats) over the council fathers in order to yield his own desired outcome, at a fundamental level he had no authority on doctrinal questions. The emperor's decree had no authoritative bearing on how the Church received the teachings of a council.

The teaching authority possessed by the Church was granted her by Christ, as we have seen. The emperor does not have this authority. It is invested in the apostles and their successors, the bishops throughout the world teaching in union with the pope. So, regardless of the role played by the emperor with respect to a given council, it is the bishops and the pope whose actions really matter.

Let's take an historical example to illustrate the role the emperors usually played, in reality, which is contrary in many ways to the prevailing narrative. Many people—including many historians—are under the impression that Constantine pressured bishops to accept the doctrine of the Trinity as described at the Council of Nicaea. Some even say that he was responsible for creating the doctrine out of thin air himself, or at least played a part in such a fabrication. However, Constantine's concern at the council was not doctrinal. What he wanted was a quick and definitive settlement of the question, and resolution to the Arian controversy that was causing such problems throughout the empire. He wanted to avoid division in the Church and strife in the empire. He did not grasp the magnitude of the questions at hand, as can be seen in a letter he sent to the heretic Arius. All he wanted was some resolution of the question. The doctrinal work of the council was still done by the bishops themselves, and, of course, the final call lay in the hands of the pope.

24. Where do the names of councils come from?

Councils take their names from the location where the council is held—thus, each of the Councils of Nicaea was held in that city; the two Vatican Councils were held in the Vatican; etc. This can cause some confusion, as we will see in the case of the Council of Basel/Ferrara/Florence! (see question 62)

25. Does the pope have to attend a council?

No, he does not. Historically, the pope typically sent representatives (legates) in his stead, whether to preside over the council or at least to participate. However, in order for a council to be considered "ecumenical", it must be confirmed and ratified by the pope.

26. Can an ecumenical council err in defining a matter pertaining to faith and morals?

No, the bishops teaching in concert with the Holy Father, defining Church teaching on matters of faith and morals, are protected by the Holy Spirit from teaching error. Of course, this does not mean that any disciplinary decisions made by a council cannot be changed in the future. The council teaching in union with the pope has supreme authority in all matters, and even matters *other than* faith and morals the council teaches authoritatively, if not definitively. But the protection from teaching error pertains only to definitions on matters of faith and morals. According to *Lumen Gentium*, when bishops meet in an ecumenical council, it is even more clear that they teach infallibly (see *Lumen Gentium* 25).

27. Do Protestants adhere to the councils?

This is a bit of a complicated question to answer. While most Protestants accept the truth of what the early councils taught, they do not accept the *authority* of these councils. In other words, if you were to ask a Protestant why they believe that Jesus was fully God and fully man, as explained and defined by the Christological councils, they would not say it was because the councils taught it.

So the question arises: What does a Protestant even think a council is? What sort of authority do those early councils have?

The principle of *sola scriptura* is one of the foundational tenets of Protestant Christianity: Scripture is the sole infallible rule of faith, they say, so no council, no gathering of bishops (or anyone else, for that matter), can solemnly define or declare anything binding. The Council fathers do not have any *ex officio* teaching authority; rather, the authority of the early councils' teachings comes from the fact that these councils teach sound biblical theology. In other words, the councils have authority because they got it right, by their estimation. Of course, this ignores Christ's granting of the power to "bind and loose" to the apostles (see Mt 16 and 18), his mandate to them to go out into the world preaching and teaching (see Mt 28), Saint Paul's instruction to adhere to his teaching whether by word of mouth or by letter (see 2 Thess 2:15), and the precedent set in the Acts of the Apostles at the so-called Council of Jerusalem (more on that below).

Officially, just about every Protestant community would

say it accepts the teachings of the first four ecumenical councils, and some would even say the first seven.

28. Did the Nicene Creed come from a council?

The proper name for the Nicene Creed in its current form is the Niceno-Constantinopolitan Creed. This creed was formulated at the First Council of Nicaea in A.D. 325, utilizing the basic form of the Apostles' Creed and the declaration of faith during the rite of baptism; the creed was then added to at the First Council of Constantinople in A.D. 381. There was one significant addition after this, when the term *filioque* ("and the son") was added, indicating that the Holy Spirit proceeds, not just from the Father, but from the Son as well.

29. Is a council just for discussions and meetings? In this day and age, can't this all be accomplished over email or video calls? What's the difference?

There have always been remote means of communication. Today we have letters, email, video conferencing, and telephone. Two thousand years ago it was only letters. But such is not a convocation; there is no "convening" if communications are done remotely like this. There is something very different about meeting in person, as opposed to some sort of remote or virtual communication. Among other things, a council involves much more than simply communicating information from one party to another—there are countless meetings, discussions, conversations. More importantly and fundamentally, there is

communal prayer, the Holy Sacrifice of the Mass celebrated by all the bishops together with the pope. There
are the after-hours conversations over dinner or drinks.
This would simply not be possible in a remote or virtual
setting. Additionally, there is something to be said for
the way the Holy Spirit acts in us when we are physically
gathered together. Our Lord told us, "For where two or
three are gathered in my name, there am I in the midst
of them" (Mt 18:20).

30. What is the point of a Church council?

Each of the twenty-one (so far) ecumenical councils has
been called in response to some need, some challenge being faced by the Church. As we will see below, when we
look at the historical context for each council, the issue
being addressed has usually been some heretical teaching
that is spreading in popularity, leading people astray. But
sometimes it is not as clear as that, and the council fathers must address an issue with fuzzier boundaries. In
any event, the point of an ecumenical council is to address a challenge faced by the Church, to find a solution to some problem. Each council has its own unique
purpose, based on the circumstances that led to its being
called in the first place. The bishops of the world meet
to discuss and resolve these problems. They meet in order to discuss and address the issue and to teach *in unison*, together with the pope. It is a serious and profound
statement of the Church's teaching authority and of the
responsibility the bishops have, as the successors of the

apostles, to teach authoritatively on matters of faith and morals and to shepherd the souls in their care.

So while every council has its own unique context, one could say that *every* council is called in order to protect, defend, and proclaim the faith, the splendor of truth that is safeguarded by the Catholic Church.

31. Are the Orthodox bishops still invited to ecumenical councils?

As we shall see in our historical examination of the councils, the relations with the Orthodox have played a significant role at many of the Church's ecumenical councils. After a brief reunion following the Fourth Lateran Council and the Council of Basel/Ferrara/Florence, the Orthodox were invited to the First Vatican Council (1869–1870), although none attended; they were also invited to the Second Vatican Council as observers. Initially, only the Russian Orthodox sent observers, but others joined in later council sessions. While they were not participating with a vote, they could participate in some discussions, and their presence and involvement still influenced the council's proceedings.

Because of advances in the ecumenical movement, and the Church's vastly improved relations with many of the autocephalous churches in the Orthodox communion, there is little question that Orthodox bishops would be invited to a new ecumenical council. They would likely be invited to observe, and perhaps even to participate in discussions and debates, but that all depends on the state of Catholic-Orthodox relations at that time.

32. Have non-Catholic, non-Orthodox ever participated in councils?

Yes; of course, this would not really have been a thing prior to the Council of Trent, which was called in response to the Protestant Reformation. There are, of course, non-Catholics who are not Protestants or Eastern Orthodox, such as the Coptic church in Egypt, the Armenian Apostolic church, the Ethiopian Orthodox church, and more. German Protestants were invited to the Council of Trent—and the location of that council was chosen in large part to make their attendance more convenient—although none took up the offer. Nearly one hundred representatives of Protestant communions took up the offer of Saint John XXIII to participate in the Second Vatican Council. They did not have voting power, of course, but their attendance and participation in some small way was an important ecumenical gesture.

33. Are councils closed and confidential, like a conclave to elect the pope, or are they public events?

There are some aspects of the council's business that are done in private. If anything, this might be purely to give the council fathers a chance to work with a little of the pressure taken off and to try to avoid some of the possible coercion that can come from being under a microscope, so to speak. It can be difficult to have a truly open discussion or debate, especially on a controversial topic, directly in the public eye. But don't picture a council as operating like a conclave, in extreme secrecy under penalty of excommunication.

In the years since the Second Vatican Council, the most recent ecumenical council, we have seen the advent of the internet, smart phones, the twenty-four-hour news cycle, social media, and more, which allow for instantaneous communication of information around the world. There's no question that in the past, the majority of the world's population—indeed, even the majority of Catholics—had no idea a council was happening, let alone any interest in the day-to-day proceedings. The Second Vatican Council was met with worldwide fascination, and any future council would see scrutiny and dissemination of information we've never seen before.

34. Are there councils that Catholics, Orthodox, Protestants, and other Christians (Copts, Anglicans, etc.) all universally accept?

There is a tremendous variety of Christian churches, and among them there is a great deal of disagreement about the legitimacy of ecumenical councils.

When it comes to Protestant communities, there is so much variation that it is impossible to say that "all Protestants" agree on just about anything, including their opinion and assessment of the councils. That being said, the vast majority of Protestants, Orthodox, and other Christians do accept the first four councils, and many even the first seven.

The Assyrian Church of the East split from the mainstream Church at the Council of Ephesus in A.D. 431

and, to this day, accepts the authority of only the first two councils. It is fair to say that all Christians universally accept the Council of Nicaea and the First Council of Constantinople, while most accept the first four or even seven.

35. Why do the Protestants accept only the first four or seven as ecumenical?

As discussed in the answer to question 27, most Protestants recognize the first four or seven ecumenical councils as being authoritative because those councils got it right, in their eyes. The teachings of those councils, they say, reflect sound biblical theology. Those councils taught fundamental Christian teaching, so they are regarded as being normative and foundational. If a council does not teach what Protestants regard as sound teaching, that council is not considered authoritative.

36. Why do the Orthodox accept only the first seven as ecumenical?

The dispute between the Catholic and Orthodox churches essentially comes down to a question of authority, and specifically the authority of the pope in relation to all other bishops around the world. In the Orthodox view, after the first seven ecumenical councils, the Catholic Church took it upon herself to proceed unilaterally, and the pope acted above and beyond his rightful authority, without proper deference to the chief patriarchs of the East. As a result of this, they do not consider any of the subsequent councils as "ecumenical", as in their view they are essentially "councils of the West".

37. *Apart from councils and synods, there are many other ways in which bishops gather together to teach as a group: within a state; within a region; within a country; within a continent; within a language group, etc. How is this different from a council?*

As we have seen, the Church's teaching authority was given to her by Christ, through the teaching office of the apostles and their successors, the bishops. The fullest expression of the teaching office of the bishops is an ecumenical council, when the bishops of the world all join together to teach in union with the pope, the successor of Saint Peter, the prince of the apostles.

But each bishop, by virtue of his office, is the primary teacher of the faith in his diocesan territory. When bishops of a given region (whether state, region, country, continent, etc.) gather together to teach in common, there is more supernatural authority to their teaching, but it is a profound sign of unity in the faith.

All bishops, or a group of bishops teaching together, have their particular magisterium, the body of teaching that comes from them. Of course, they are not free to teach innovations, but must adhere to the deposit of faith.

Each bishop has authority over his own flock and can teach authoritatively; similarly, bishops together in a region can teach together in a profound sign of the Church's unity beyond diocesan boundaries. The teachings of bishops united together have a certain gravity to them, and this can be seen most dramatically in the infallibility that is enjoyed by *all* of the bishops teaching together under certain circumstances.

38. I've heard of "pontifical councils". Are these anything like ecumenical councils?

No, a "pontifical council" is a sort of department (or "dicastery") in the Vatican. These are typically led by an archbishop or a cardinal and assist the pope (and work at his behest) in certain areas of the Church's life. They are not deliberative, teaching assemblies of the bishops and so, in that sense, are completely unrelated to the councils we are examining in this book. As of June 5, 2022, pontifical councils are referred to as dicasteries, as are the former Vatican congregations.

HISTORICAL QUESTIONS

39. What are the "pre-ecumenical councils"?

There are a number of councils that predate the Council of Nicaea, which we have seen is considered the first truly ecumenical council. The most famous example is the so-called Council of Jerusalem, which we read about in the Acts of the Apostles (see question 42). Quite simply, they are called "pre-ecumenical" because they predate the first truly ecumenical council, Nicaea in 325.

40. What sort of weight did/do these have?

These councils do not have the same weight as an ecumenical council; the universal Church is not held to their decrees as with an ecumenical council. We have seen above how an ecumenical council is the fullest manifestation of the bishops of the world teaching together in union with the pope, which is what gives an ecumenical council the supreme level of authority that it has. The pre-ecumenical councils, while each was important in its own way, do not meet this standard.

41. Did any of these have lasting effects that come down to us today?

The most prominent effect of the pre-ecumenical councils would be their contribution to the establishment of the *structure* for future debates within the Church. Particularly in the Council of Jerusalem (see below), we see a clear model of collegiality and synodality, as it might be called today, with Peter as the undisputed head. There is spirited debate among the apostles and others, with two primary camps forming; and how is the question ultimately resolved? By appeal to Peter's authority. The apostles know quite well that Peter is the keeper of the keys, the "rock" on which Christ built his Church (Mt 16:18). They know that, while they were all tasked with teaching the faith and spreading the gospel to the whole world, Peter has a particular role of primacy even among the apostles. So they appeal to his authority, and he makes the final call. This basic structure of debate, discussion, and decision would guide the Church from that point on.

42. What happened at the Council of Jerusalem?

The so-called "Council of Jerusalem" was an episode in the very early life of the Church. The events are related to us in the fifteenth chapter of the Acts of the Apostles and the second chapter of Saint Paul's letter to the Galatians.

By this time, the missionary efforts of the apostles were having a great effect among both Jews and Gentiles. In particular, Peter and Paul were bringing great numbers —especially Gentiles—into the fold. Up to this point, the followers of Christ had been almost exclusively Jews. The Messiah had come, so it makes sense that his first followers would be those who had been *waiting for* the Messiah for so many centuries. Jesus came to fulfill the law; he was the promised Messiah; his followers did not see themselves as some new religion but, rather, as the logical continuation of (and even completion, *fulfillment of*) Judaism. So when great numbers of Gentiles began joining the Church, important and thorny questions—both theological and practical—arose.

The trickiest question was this: Are Christians (whether Jew or Gentile) obligated to adhere to the Mosaic law? The primary concerns here would have been dietary restrictions and circumcision. The Circumcision Party, or "Judaizers", said that Christians had to adhere to the Mosaic law to the letter. As so often happens, another group formed, under the guidance of Peter and Paul, who held that Christians were not beholden to the Mosaic law.

When Peter went to Antioch, he would not eat with the Gentile converts; even though he did not think they were obliged to follow the Mosaic law, apparently he was attempting to satisfy the Circumcision Party, meaning treating the Gentile converts as ritualistically unclean. Paul rebuked Peter for this, as we see in the second chapter of the letter to the Galatians. The Christians in Antioch sent Paul and others to Jerusalem to try to come to some sort of agreement on the matter.

James the Lesser, one of the twelve apostles who at the time was Bishop of Jerusalem, evidently sort of led the group who thought all Christians—even non-Jews who became Christians—needed to adhere to the Mosaic law. When the apostles and others met in council, Peter presided, and at the end they all agreed that Christians were not obliged to follow the Mosaic law. The apostles sent a letter to Antioch explaining the results of their discernment: "It has seemed good to the Holy Spirit and to us to lay upon you no greater burden than these necessary things" (Acts 15:28A).

43. Why is this not considered an ecumenical council?

As we have seen, there are certain criteria that have to be met for a council to be considered "ecumenical". One of these is that it is attended by the bishops of the world, from all regions, and is approved as ecumenical by the pope. The so-called Council of Jerusalem, one could say, is on a level all its own: it is sometimes called the Apostolic Council, because the apostles themselves participated in it. Catholics recognize the bishops as the successors to the apostles, but as this was attended by the apostles themselves, it is on another level altogether.

44. What prompted the First Council of Nicaea, and what happened?

In A.D. 325, the Emperor Constantine called for a council to be held in Nicaea. A priest named Arius, living in Alexandria, was teaching that Jesus Christ was not God, but something less, while at the same time something more than man. Arius taught that Jesus was the greatest creation of God, but thus still just a creature. This of course differed from orthodox Catholic teaching, but at this point that teaching had not been clearly articulated. Constantine's advisors suggested a council, so that the teaching could be defined and the errors of Arius defeated.

The number of bishops in attendance is a surprisingly controversial question, with some sources reporting as few as 200, but the generally accepted number is 318 out of about 1800 bishops in the world at the time. There were only five from the Western empire. While Pope Sylvester I (r. 314–335) did not attend the Council of Nicaea, he did approve the emperor's calling of this council, and he sent delegates as his representatives.

Keep in mind the historical context in which this council took place: just a dozen years earlier in A.D. 313, the Edict of Milan made it legal to be Christian in the Roman Empire and ended the official persecutions. Some of the bishops in attendance at Nicaea had suffered a great deal under the emperor Diocletian, even to the point of being maimed and scarred. Constantine greeted these men with joy, kissing their wounds. This shows the remarkable faith of the emperor, although his motivations in calling this council were primarily political: his concern was with maintaining peace in the empire.

To say that Constantine's primary concern was the unity of the empire is not to say that he was indifferent to orthodoxy, but his pragmatism in regard to the empire's survival would win the day. He just wanted some sort of resolution of the debate, which he hoped would then lead to homogeneity of belief and, more importantly, a cooling of the conflict. Once it was clear that the bishops were landing on the side of the orthodox Catholic position, Constantine applied pressure to the dissenting bishops so that they would agree.

Constantine was not alone in his desire for imperial peace and unity. There were even some "semi-Arian" bishops who were sympathetic to the Arian cause but wanted compromise and peace and an end to the conflict more than anything.

At the council's invitation, Arius himself presented his teachings to the council fathers, and his position was then hotly debated. It was decided that a creed would be drafted, a written statement of belief. The driving force behind this was as a corrective to Arius' position that Jesus was created—to correct this, the creed included the line "Genitum, non factum, consubstantialem Patri" (Begotten, not made, consubstantial with the Father). The Greek equivalent of *consubstantialem* was *homoousios* ("of the same substance"), as opposed to *homoiousios* ("of similar substance"). Part of the debate involved differences in understanding of the terminology between the Eastern and Western bishops, but in the end the traditional orthodox position won out: the Son is fully divine, not a creature. Of the 318 bishops in attendance, 316 voted in favor of the text of the creed; the two who refused were sent into exile.

The council also produced many canons that were disciplinary rather than doctrinal, including the deposition of clerics who practice usury, prohibitions on deacons distributing the Eucharist to priests, and more.

One interesting point about Nicaea that is often neglected is a way that it emphasized Roman primacy and the primacy of the successor of Peter. The council fathers declared that Rome's calculations for the date of Easter should be the standard that all other churches should follow. This was a profound statement on the part of the council that Rome holds primacy and that Rome should be the standard on such matters. One could almost say that the council was applying just the second half of Saint Ambrose's famous advice to Saint Monica: "Do as the Romans do."

While the Church unequivocally condemned Arius' ideas at the council, shortly thereafter these ideas would resurface and gain traction yet again, and in the eyes of some Arius would even be rehabilitated. Some of the emperors even supported the Arians. This would cause great problems for the Church going forward and would even result in the calling of additional ecumenical councils.

45. Did Saint Nicholas really slap Arius at the First Council of Nicaea?

There is a story you may have heard that Saint Nicholas, bishop of Myra (in modern-day Turkey), slapped the infamous heretic Arius at the Council of Nicaea for his heterodox teachings and for leading so many astray from the true Catholic faith.

While the story is certainly a dramatic one (and there are some variations that make it even more dramatic), it is almost certainly apocryphal. The earliest record we have of the story is from the fourteenth century, a full millennium after the council. This in itself does not necessarily mean the story is untrue, of course. Without evidence, it is dubious to rely on a claim a thousand years removed! But the main point of the tale is to emphasize the orthodoxy of Saint Nicholas and the passion with which he defended the faith. *That* is something we should all emulate.

46. What prompted the First Council of Constantinople, and what happened?

The First Council of Constantinople was held in A.D. 381, under Pope Damasus and Emperor Theodosius I. It was attended by around 150 bishops. This council was called in response to a heresy that was being spread by the followers of a man named Macedonius, who belittled the divinity of the Holy Spirit, as well as to the persistence of Arianism in spite of the Nicene condemnations of that heresy.

The Arians' errors pertained not only to the person of the Son, but to the Holy Spirit as well. They believed that the Holy Spirit was not of the same substance as the Father (or the Son) and that he was not co-eternal with them. As these errors spread and gained traction, the Church knew a response was needed.

This council added to the creed that was previously composed at the First Council of Nicaea. The portions added, in response to Macedonius and his followers, concerned the Holy Spirit, and all the following lines until the end of the creed, as we have it in its present form. This is why the full name of the creed is the Niceno-Constantinopolitan Creed. In fact, because of the number of bishops involved in this council, the creed was at times called "the faith of the 150 fathers".

Saint Gregory Nazianzen—Church father, Doctor of the Church—was elected bishop of Constantinople during the council and ended up presiding over it for a time. However, he was immediately challenged by a vocal opposition; the opposition was so great and disruptive that Gregory eventually resigned.

As we have seen, while the council was convened during the reign of Pope Damasus, it was actually a general synod of the East, so the pope did not have a presence here, not even through legates. Damasus approved of the council at the time, but it did not receive its "ecumenical" status until later popes ratified its decrees for the universal Church.

This council also helped to solidify Rome as the center of the Catholic Christian world and the bishop of Rome as the supreme authority in the Church. It helped that Rome was always on the side of orthodoxy and did not produce any major heresies that became associated with the city. Constantinople was declared to be a sort of second-place see, but the pope did not affirm this canon.

Pagan worship was also made illegal by the council, in collaboration with the emperor himself. The council also said that the destruction of pagan temples was allowed, although this part appears not to have been enforced by the emperor. Here, once again, we see the union of religion and empire under Theodosius, only this time under Christian auspices. Through the Edict of Thessalonica just the year before, Theodosius had made Christianity the official state religion—and, thus, the only legal religion in the empire. Even Constantine had previously promoted the concept of religious liberty, but those days were long gone. "Separation of Church and State" would have been completely foreign to the mind of Theodosius.

One final note about the creed that flowed from these first two ecumenical councils: in the West, the Holy Spirit is described as proceeding "from the Father and the Son". This "and the Son" in Latin is *filioque*, and this term was not added to the creed until many years after this council. It was the result of further discernment of the nature of the Trinity and how the Holy Spirit relates to the Father and the Son. The East did not adopt this term, so the Niceno-Constantinopolitan Creed as recited in the Christian East still says, "I believe in the Holy Spirit, the Lord, the giver of life, who proceeds from the Father." The addition of this term was tremendously controversial in the East and is a source of theological tension to this day.

47. What prompted the Council of Ephesus, and what happened?

The next ecumenical council was held in A.D. 431, in the City of Ephesus, in modern-day Turkey. Attended by more than 200 bishops, the council was presided over by Saint Cyril of Alexandria, as the representative of Pope Saint Celestine I (r. 422–432). Saint Cyril was the obvious choice to lead the council's proceedings, as the controversy that led to the council saw Cyril as the staunchest defender of orthodox belief.

Perhaps this council's most significant contribution to the elucidation of Church teaching was its declaration of Mary as *theotokos* (Greek for "God bearer", thus "Mother of God"). This was an incredibly important development, as it helped to define the divinity of Jesus Christ as well as the unity of the person of Jesus—there is no separation between Jesus the man and the Divine Second Person of the Blessed Trinity. There is one man, who is both human and divine. Thus, as Mary was the Mother of Jesus

Christ, who is God, she is the Mother of God. While this is ostensibly a definition of a doctrine about Mary, fundamentally it is actually about the person of Jesus Christ.

This teaching was in response to the heresy being spread by Nestorius, who was at the time the bishop of Constantinople. Nestorianism was spreading through the Church, and his position as bishop of such an important see certainly played a role in the spread of his erroneous teaching.

Nestorius had a reputation as a gifted preacher and holy priest, and as the new patriarch of Constantinople at Christmas in A.D. 428, he preached vehemently against the title *Theotokos* for the Blessed Virgin Mary. He said she should not be called "Mother of God" because God could have no mother, since the creature cannot bear and give birth to the creator. Nestorius preached that the body of the man that was carried in Mary's womb was assumed by God, taken over and utilized for the Incarnation. Of course, this is an attack, not on Mary, but on the nature of Jesus Christ. Nestorius' inability to reconcile the seeming contradiction of the creature giving birth to the creator led him to coin the term *Christotokos*—Christ-bearer. Saint Cyril of Alexandria wrote to Nestorius to correct him in charity, imploring him to accept the orthodox teaching of the Church on this matter. Nestorius refused, so Cyril wrote to the emperor and Pope Saint Celestine I to seek counsel before publicly condemning Nestorius. The pope confirmed Cyril's sense that Nestorius' stance was not in accord with the faith, and an ecumenical council was convened to address the matter. The council would proceed with no small amount of political and personal intrigue among the bishops, but for our purposes here, it is enough to discuss the end results of the council.

The way in which the Second Vatican Council grabbed the world's attention was not unique to that council. Perhaps the worldwide reach was a new phenomenon, but people have sometimes eagerly awaited the decisions of ecumenical councils since the earliest days of the Church. At Ephesus, huge throngs of people waited outside the building where the council's proceedings were taking place to hear its decisions. Saint Cyril wrote that the people cried out in praise of God when they heard that orthodoxy had won the day and Nestorius had been deposed, and they walked in procession with the council fathers as they departed.

Of course, as in so many cases, the council's deliberations and decisions did not end the matter. The political struggles continued. Various factions disputed each other's findings and would hold counter-councils in opposition to Ephesus, even writing to the emperor to declare that *their* council was the *real* one and that he should throw his support behind *them*. In the end, the emperor accepted the original (and true) council's teachings. Nestorius was deposed by the council, at first he was allowed to retire, but when he refused to hold his tongue and continued teaching heresy, he was exiled.

The followers of Nestorius persist to this day, in some form. They prefer not to be called "Nestorians", and some (like the Assyrian Church of the East) have even officially recognized the term *Theotokos* and the primacy of the pope. They do not accept the Council of Ephesus, let alone any of the ecumenical councils that would follow.

48. What prompted the Council of Chalcedon, and what happened?

The Council of Chalcedon was convened in A.D. 451, under Pope Saint Leo the Great and Emperor Marcian. It was attended by more than 500 bishops, making it the most well-attended council up to that time. A man named Eutyches denied Jesus' true human nature, and of course his errors were spreading rapidly. In contrast and correction to Eutyches' errors, the council affirmed that the two natures of Christ—human and divine—are united in one Divine Person, without confusion, without separation. But let's unpack that context a bit.

The Council of Chalcedon flowed naturally from the Council of Ephesus in that it was partially meant to address some of that council's shortcomings, in a manner of speaking. The Emperor Theodosius had called a "Second Council of Ephesus" in A.D. 449, intended to resolve theological issues that had arisen in the eighteen years since the first council in that city. A monk named Eutyches was teaching that Jesus had two natures prior to the Incarnation, but only one afterward—in other words, that his human and divine natures were melded into one. He said that Jesus' human nature was absorbed into his divine nature, leaving only the one in the end—the heresy would come to be known as *monophysitism* (one nature). The problem here, of course, is that if the human nature of Jesus was *absorbed into* his divine nature, then he was not fully human.[1] Eutyches was denounced by Flavian, the patriarch of Constantinople. Eutyches' followers took over this so-called "Second Council of Ephesus", supported his teaching, and voted to exile Flavian. Pope Leo was furious when he heard about this travesty of justice and scathingly described the "council" as "non judicium, sed latrocinium" (not a judicial gathering, but a council of robbers).

In response to the heresies of Eutyches, Pope Saint Leo the Great wrote a massive letter to Flavian (now known as the *Tome* of Leo) explaining the Church's orthodox teaching on the natures of Christ,[2] and thought that the matter was settled.[3] He intended for this letter to be read during the Second Council of Ephesus' proceedings, but it was not, and as a result it did not have its intended effect of clearing up confusion and resolving the situation. The emperor was sympathetic to Eutyches, and he made sure that the council fathers threw their support behind Eutyches, in opposition to Flavian and Leo. This is why the council is not considered ecumenical: not only was it not confirmed and accepted by the pope, but Leo explicitly condemned it as a "council of robbers".

---

[1] As was often the case with the Christological heresies, Eutyches had good intentions but was misguided. He wanted to defend against the erroneous notion that Jesus was *two persons*, but was overzealous in his defense, yielding the monophysite heresy.

[2] This is technically known as the "hypostatic union": Jesus Christ is one Divine Person with two natures, human and divine, which are without confusion, change, division, or separation.

[3] This is a clear example of Leo's understanding of papal primacy. As the successor of Saint Peter, he saw himself as responsible for ensuring orthodox belief and teaching throughout the universal Church, not merely in his own local diocese.

Leo wanted a new council to be convened, this time in the West so that he could attend and oversee it. (Here we see another example of Leo's understanding of the primacy of the papacy and the definitive role the pope plays in ecclesiastical and doctrinal matters.) The emperor did convene a new council, but not in the West—he chose Chalcedon, which was close to Constantinople, Flavian's see. This time, Leo sent delegates who would not be pushed around, and his *Tome* was read at the council, after which the bishops cried out, "Peter has spoken through Leo!"

In addition to approving Leo's *Tome* and a "Definition of Faith" that detailed the Church's orthodox teaching on Christ and reiterated the teachings of the previous councils, the fathers also approved nearly thirty disciplinary canons.

The Council of Chalcedon has one particular black eye in its reputation. For the first time in the Church's history, there was a division or schism in the Church that continues down to the present day. The differences between Latin and Greek led to some extreme difficulty in hammering out and defining the union of Jesus' two natures; this problem was exacerbated by certain bishops' desires to be politically expedient rather than theologically accurate. The two groups declared heretical by the council were strong enough to endure the council's condemnations and continue to this day as distinct ecclesial groups. Specifically, the Assyrian Church of the East today traces its lineage back to Nestorius of Constantinople, who taught too much separation between Christ's natures; and the Oriental Orthodox (or Coptic) church today started when Dioscorus of Alexandria, who along with Eutyches' followers proposed too *little* separation between the natures of Christ, split from the mainstream Church. Both groups' understandings of the person of Christ and the relation of the two natures was condemned by the majority of bishops at the council, and each group thought that the mainstream decision veered too closely to the other end of the spectrum!

Remarkably, and on a hopeful note, both of these groups were reconciled with the Catholic Church in the twentieth century. While they and the Catholic Church acknowledge each other as non-heretical, they are still considered "non-Chalcedonian" churches and distinct ecclesial bodies.

49. Do the councils always finally resolve the issues they confront?

While the decrees of ecumenical councils (in response to heresies or other issues in the life of the Church) are meant to give a solution, a definitive answer, to a problem, seldom does this act definitively and immediately resolve the issue. It is not hard to understand why: no one likes to be corrected, and no one likes to be told he is wrong. When the Church declares a given teaching heretical, the adherents of that teaching are unlikely to acquiesce immediately and change their ways. On the contrary, in some cases it causes them to dig in their heels. However, the Church's decree does often stop the *spread* of these erroneous teachings.

As we have seen, following the Council of Nicaea's

(and subsequent councils') condemnation of Arianism, that particular heresy was still alive and well and even thrived for many, many years to come. In fact, a breed of Arianism still runs rampant today. There was also the case we saw at the Council of Chalcedon, whose condemned theologies remain today in the Assyrian Church of the East and the Oriental Orthodox Church (although, as we saw in the answer to question 48, these theologies were reconciled with the Catholic teaching in the twentieth century). Of course, probably the most obvious example would be the resiliency of Protestantism following the Council of Trent.

50. What prompted the Second Council of Constantinople, and what happened?

The Second Council of Constantinople was convened in A.D. 553 by Pope Vigilius and Emperor Justinian I. Around 165 bishops were in attendance. This council confirmed the first four ecumenical councils, which was particularly important in the context of the Council of Chalcedon.

The emperor and the pope were engaged in an epic power struggle. The emperor insisted that his power extended not only over secular matters but over theological and doctrinal matters, as well. At this point, even after so many councils hammering out the orthodox Christian understanding of the person of Jesus Christ and the nature of the Trinity, there was a great deal of dissent.

As we have seen, the Council of Chalcedon fought against the heresy of *monophysitism*, which said that Jesus had only one nature, a divine one, and thus denied Jesus' human nature. However, the monophysites did not disappear overnight and even had some adherents in high places. Justinian (r. 527–565) became emperor after the death of his uncle, Justin (r. 518–527). He wanted to end the theological division and fighting between the Monophysites and orthodox Christianity. His wife, Theodora, was an avowed Monophysite and even kept a group of Monophysite monks in a community at the palace. Theodora's adherence, of course, influenced her husband's position, but first and foremost Justinian wanted to end the argument that was consuming the empire.

Justinian viewed the emperor, rather than the pope, as Christ's vicar, and so it was his responsibility to settle the doctrinal matter. This view clashed, to say the least, with that of the pope. But we will come back to that in a moment.

One reason for the continued conflict with the Monophysites was that they viewed the Council of Chalcedon's work as incomplete. While the council did condemn Nestorius and his views, it did not condemn three others who influenced Nestorius: Theodore of Mopsuestia; Theodoret of Cyrus; and Ibas of Edessa. The Monophysites saw this oversight as an implicit statement of support of these thinkers. Justinian issued an edict that affirmed Chalcedon's teachings and condemned these writings, which were known as the Three Chapters. He thought this would mend the rift between the Monophysites and Orthodox Christians, as he believed the Monophysites were not heretics, but were only misunderstood. Naturally, the Monophysites appreciated this move, but the Orthodox saw it as an overstepping of the emperor's proper authority, encroaching on matters that were properly under the purview of the pope. Furthermore, it was not the emperor's place to modify the work of an ecumenical council by imperial edict. The edict was sent to Rome for approval.

Pope Vigilius (r. 537–555) was an ambitious man. As papal legate to Constantinople, he had befriended Theodora in the hopes that this would help his papal ambitions. He thought he would succeed Pope Agipatus (r. 535–536), but Silverius (r. 536–537) was elected instead. Vigilius, enraged at what he saw as an injustice, collaborated with a general who arrested and imprisoned Silverius, after which Vigilius was elected. Of course, Silverius was technically still the pope as he had not abdicated; however Silverius died in December of 537. At that point Vigilius was universally acknowledged as pope. He is not considered an anti-pope.

Vigilius saw Justinian's edict as a problematic encroachment and refused to approve the edict or to come to Constantinople to discuss. Justinian had Vigilius arrested during Mass in Rome and brought to Constantinople, where he was imprisoned for a decade. Eventually he agreed to condemn the Three Chapters, but many of the Western bishops did not agree with him. So far, Justinian's actions had not done anything to solve the conflict!

Ultimately, the emperor agreed to Vigilius' suggestion to hold an ecumenical council to resolve the matter. The council was held in Constantinople in 553. The Three Chapters were condemned, and the teachings of the previous councils were reiterated and reaffirmed. Following the council, Vigilius was released by the emperor and allowed to return to Rome, but died on the way.

The Third Council of Constantinople was held from A.D. 680 to 681, under Popes Agatho and Leo II and Emperor Constantine IV. It was attended by 174 bishops and patriarchs, including the Patriarch of Constantinople and Patriarch of Antioch. The emperor was also in attendance, even presiding at the first eleven sessions.

This council was Christological in nature and arose in response to the heresy of *monothelitism* (the belief that Christ had only one will). The Patriarch of Constantinople, Sergius, tried to counter the Monophysite heresy by proposing that Christ only had one will, a divine will. What Sergius did not see was that such a claim denies the full humanity of Jesus, which of course had been defined at earlier Church councils. Sergius tried to drum up the support of the pope, Honorius (r. 625–638), who provided an ambiguous response. The controversy swept far and wide, to the point that Emperor Heraclius (r. 610–641) even tried to assert his authority in the doctrinal realm, declaring Monothelitism as doctrine even though he hadn't the authority to do so.

In 649, Pope Martin I (r. 649–655) called for a meeting of bishops at the Lateran Palace in Rome to discuss the heresy of Monothelitism. Patriarch Paul II of Constantinople was excommunicated for his role in spreading the heresy, which led Emperor Constans II (r. 641–668) to try to get rid of the pope. A plot was hatched wherein a swordsman would go to Mass and strike the pope dead at communion; miraculously, however, when the moment came, the would-be assassin could not see the pope. Martin was kidnapped and imprisoned on an island in the Aegean Sea a few years later.[4]

Martin was brought back to Constantinople in late 654 and spent three months in jail and was later tried for numerous trumped-up charges, although the real reason for all of this was his refusal to support Monothelitism. He was sentenced to death, publicly humiliated, and tortured, but the emperor decided to exile him instead to Crimea, where he died. Pope Saint Martin I is considered the last martyred pope.

The story thus far is remarkable and (as is so often the case) filled with a great deal of drama and intrigue. Twenty-five years after Martin's death, Emperor Constantine IV (r. 652–685) called the Third Council of Constantinople, which Pope Saint Agatho (r. 678–681) approved. The primary order of business was the condemnation of Monothelitism, which the council fathers vociferously accomplished. Pope Saint Leo II (r. 681–683) succeeded Agatho while the council was in session. The council had also condemned Pope Honorius as a heretic in dramatic terms, but Leo altered that decree, explaining that Honorius had the opportunity to condemn the heresy but did not; he let heresy continue, which was negligent but not heretical.

The council produced a statement of faith that built off of those at the First Councils of Nicaea and Constantinople.

---

[4] Here we have an interesting and somewhat confusing situation: after a year, the clergy of Rome elected a new pope, Eugenius I, as they assumed Martin must be dead. However, Martin was still very much alive, which meant Eugenius was not really the pope, but he was acting as a sort of caretaker or administrator. When Martin did eventually die in 655, Eugenius succeeded him.

The Second Council of Nicaea was held in A.D. 786–787, convoked by Emperor Constantine VI and his mother, Irene (as Constantine was a minor, Irene was acting as regent), during the reign of Pope Adrian I. Adrian sent legates to Nicaea, who presided over the council. Sources vary, but the council was attended by somewhere between 300 and 367 bishops.

A dispute had arisen in the eighth century regarding the veneration and use of icons and other holy images. Emperor Leo III (r. 717–741) thought that a volcanic eruption in 726 was God's punishment for the idolatrous worship of icons that the emperor claimed was rampant throughout the empire. Because of this, he banned the creation of icons, which caused a massive uprising in Greece. Icons had been an important part of Christian worship for many centuries and had become a cultural touchstone particularly in the East. The emperor and his supporters were called *iconoclasts*, and thus the controversy became known as *iconoclasm*. The emperor and the pope were at odds on the matter. Pope Gregory II (r. 715–731) wrote to the emperor, explaining that the faithful do not worship icons, statues, or art, but rather that these items serve as reminders and prompt devotion to those they depict.

Unfortunately, as we have seen so many times in the Church's history, such an intervention did not put the matter to rest. The iconoclastic position had spread due to the emperor's influence, and his successor was even stricter. While Leo had ordered the destruction of icons and banned their creation, his successor, Constantine V (r. 741–775), persecuted the users of icons (known as *iconodules* or *iconophiles*). In many cases, monasteries refused to adhere to the ban, and their property was seized, and the monks and nuns were often arrested or executed. This was not viewed as a simple matter by the emperor, but as idolatry, and he reacted sternly. The matter would get more complicated with Constantine's successor, Leo VI (r. 775–780), who was himself an *iconoclast* but whose wife was not. Leo's son, Constantine VI, became emperor upon his father's death, but as he was only nine years old, his mother, Irene, ruled in his place as regent. She called for an ecumenical council, which was to be held in Nicaea, and Pope Adrian sent legates to participate.

The assembled bishops, in an effort to resolve the iconoclasm dispute, drew an important distinction between worship and reverence. Essentially, three levels of respect were identified: *latria*, which is worship, reserved to God; *hyperdulia*, the special reverence that we show to Mary because of her identity as the Mother of God; and *dulia*, the respect and reverence that we show all the saints because of our assurance that they are in heaven and that we can follow them as role models. Icons are devotional aids, the council fathers said, and as such a right treatment of them does not fall into *latria*.

The council also conducted other business and approved twenty-two canons on matters such as the election of bishops, heretical texts, the scandal caused by women living in bishops' houses or monasteries, and more.

53. What prompted the Fourth Council of Constantinople, and what happened?

The Fourth Council of Constantinople was the eighth ecumenical council and was held from A.D. 869 to 870. It was convoked by Pope Adrian II, and the emperor at the time was Basil. Accounts tell us that 102 bishops were in attendance, along with three papal legates and our patriarchs. The series of events that led to the calling of this council was intensely dramatic, with imperial decrees, mutual excommunications, bishops being deposed, emperors being killed. And this would be the final ecumenical council to be held in the East.

The primary purpose of the Fourth Council of Constantinople was to address and resolve the so-called Photian Schism. The see of Constantinople was the locus of this dispute. The Patriarch of Constantinople, Ignatius, was deposed by Emperor Michael III because he refused the emperor communion due to an accusation that the emperor had engaged in incest. The emperor placed a layman named Photius in the patriarchate, who sent a letter to the pope to announce his appointment as patriarch and introduce himself. The pope, Saint Nicholas the Great (r. 858–867), was friends with Ignatius, so he sent representatives to the emperor to see what was going on. Photius bribed the pope's representatives to give a favorable report, but the pope saw right through this and wrote a scathing letter to Photius. In the letter, the pope refused to accept Ignatius' deposition and refused to condemn him without a proper investigation; as a result, he also refused to acknowledge Photius as patriarch.

The emperor wrote to the pope and threatened to attack Rome if Photius was not recognized as patriarch, claiming that the pope did not have the authority over Church matters in Constantinople. Nicholas remained steadfast and unwavering. This is where things take a turn for the dramatic: in 867 Photius tried to exercise authority over the pope, issuing a decree of excommunication and attempting to depose the pope. Photius did not know that Nicholas had already died by this point. This effectively separated the Church in Constantinople from the pope, putting it in schism.

The drama continued, ever heightening. A month later, Emperor Michael was killed, and the new emperor reinstated Ignatius. In 869, at the suggestion of the new emperor, Basil, the new pope, Adrian II (r. 867–872), convened the Fourth Council of Constantinople. The council resolved the matter of the see of Constantinople, supporting Ignatius as patriarch and excommunicating Photius.

Later in life, Photius repented of his actions and was welcomed back into communion with the Church.

54. What prompted the First Lateran Council, and what happened?

The First Lateran Council was held in A.D. 1123 and was the first ecumenical council to be held in Rome. More than 300 bishops were in attendance, and it appears that they were all from the West. This is unsurprising, as relations between the East and West had soured greatly in the previous century, culminating in the Schism of 1054.

(The schism was the result of increasing tensions between Christians of the East and West, including disagreements over the primacy of the pope, the procession of the Holy Spirit, and more, which led to mutual excommunications by the pope and the Patriarch of Constantinople.) Convoked by Pope Callistus II (r. 1119–1124), the primary instigator of the council was what has become known as the "investiture controversy".

Briefly, the so-called "investiture controversy" arose when King Henry IV (r. 1056–1105) in Germany clashed over who had the right to give new bishops their signs of office (specifically the ring and crozier, or shepherd's staff). In Henry's realm in Germany, it was common for noblemen, who were laymen, to invest the bishop with these items, stating "Receive the Church". After swearing an oath of loyalty to this extra-ecclesial authority, the new bishop would then be ordained. Pope Gregory VII (r. 1073–1085) worried that the structure of this ceremony indicated that the secular rulers were the ones investing the bishop with his authority, when in reality it is the pope, by his authority as successor of Saint Peter, who does so.

Pope Gregory had struggled against secular rulers for his entire papacy. He felt the need to assert himself as the teacher and moral judge of secular rulers, the one to whom all secular rulers owed their own fealty and respect, the one who had the power to depose emperors and excommunicate kings if need be. Henry IV was the son and grandson of Holy Roman Emperors, a title that was granted by the act of being crowned by the pope. Henry disliked this practice and thought the pope only had authority in religious, not secular, matters. In his on-going clashes with the popes, Henry would be excommunicated five times by three different popes.

Eventually, when a conflict between Gregory and Henry over the vacant see of Milan came to a head in 1075, Gregory banned the lay investiture ceremony. In effect, he said that a bishop who received his signs of office from the hands of a layman was not a bishop and that any nobleman who did the handing over would be deposed.

Gregory tried to smooth things over when Henry reacted quite angrily to this decree, but to no avail. On Christmas Eve 1075, armed men on horseback rode into the Church of Saint Mary Major, attacked the pope in the middle of Mass, and imprisoned him in a tower. The pope was rescued in the morning by his supporters. Henry could not officially be connected to this attack, but few believed he was not the instigator.

After a brief reconciliation, Henry continued his attacks on the pope, and the conflict continued. Eventually, Pope Callistus II and King Henry V (r. 1099–1125) would agree that the ecclesiastical authorities were responsible for investing bishops, and secular authorities were responsible for investing noblemen. This agreement was ratified at the First Lateran Council in 1123.

The council fathers took up other business as well, primarily passing disciplinary canons in regard to various abuses by Church authorities. One of these abuses was simony, the buying and selling of ecclesiastical privileges.

55. What prompted the Second Lateran Council, and what happened?

The Second Lateran Council was held in A.D. 1139, the second to be held in Rome. It was convoked by Pope Innocent II (r. 1130–1143) and was attended by around 1,000 prelates as well as Emperor Conrad.

The council was called by Pope Innocent II following a period of schism in the Church. It all started in 1130 when Pope Honorius II died. A majority of the cardinals elected a man who took the name Anacletus II, and this was supported by the people of Rome. On the same day, some of the cardinals held a separate vote and elected Innocent II as pope. Innocent attempted to bolster his authority and legitimacy by holding a council in Pisa in 1135, at which he condemned Anacletus. When Anacletus died in 1138, the rift was mostly mended and Innocent was accepted as the pope. But to put a bow on the whole thing, he decided to call a council, which was to be held at the Lateran once again.

The council largely repeated and affirmed the canons of the First Lateran Council and passed a number of disciplinary canons. Many of these canons were meant to address laxity in clerical life, which the council fathers saw as an increasing problem within the Church. They tightened up and restated some of the moral requirements and expectations for clerics. In some cases it was dramatic issues like marriage and concubines among the priests, but the canons also included prohibitions on ostentatious dress among the clergy. Jousts and other such dangerous sporting tournaments were also prohibited, and physical attacks on clerics were given the punishment of excommunication.

Innocent also deposed any bishops or priests who had been ordained by Anacletus and his followers.

56. What prompted the Third Lateran Council, and what happened?

The Third Lateran Council was held in A.D. 1179, convoked by Pope Alexander III and Emperor Frederick I. The council was attended by 302 bishops, who met in Rome, and their primary concern was the healing of a schism that had arisen in the Church.

When Pope Adrian IV (r. 1154–1159) died in 1159, the cardinals met to elect his successor. Two divergent groups developed, each of which elected its own pope: one group elected Roland of Siena, who took the name Alexander III (r. 1159–1181). The other elected a man named Octavian of Rome, who won the support of the emperor even though he was elected by a smaller number of cardinals, and he took the name Victor IV.

After Victor's death, two more anti-popes would succeed him: Paschal III (1164–1168) and Callistus III (1168–1178). Alexander, however, would outlast them all, and he promised the emperor he would convene a general council to help resolve the matter.

Held in Rome in March 1179, the Third Lateran Council's primary goal would be to end the schism and reconcile the pope and emperor. About three hundred fathers from Europe and a few from the Latin East (as well as one from the Greek church) met at the Lateran. The first canon to be passed was a requirement that anyone to be regarded as Roman Pontiff must be elected by at least two-thirds of the cardinals. It did not specify how quickly the election must be completed, however, an ambiguity that would cause problems in the future.

The fathers also declared all appointments by antipopes to be invalid. Many disciplinary canons were also passed, mostly having to do with morality and civil issues.

57. What prompted the Fourth Lateran Council, and what happened?

The Fourth Lateran Council was held in A.D. 1215 and was convoked by Pope Innocent III. Over 1,200 prelates attended the council, including 71 archbishops, 412 bishops, 800 abbots, and the Primate of the Maronites (Eastern Rite Catholics, who grew out of modern-day Lebanon and Syria). It is notable that Saint Dominic and Saint Francis of Assisi were in attendance.

In 1213, Pope Innocent III (r. 1198–1216) called this council, which was to meet in 1215 at the Lateran in Rome. The purposes were many, but all boiled down to Innocent's desire to heal the Church and his recognition that even logistical, temporal problems had spiritual roots. The council was to replace vice with virtue, enact a moral reform of the Church, fight heresy, establish peace and resolve conflict, eradicate oppression, and aid the Christians in the Holy Land.

Bishops, abbots, priors, chapters, kings, and civil authorities throughout Europe were all invited. The bishops were asked to provide topics to be discussed, and only one or two bishops in each province were allowed to stay home, while the rest were obliged to attend.

The profession of faith that this council produced was formulated in a way to root out specifically the heresy of the Albigensians and Waldensians, which was overtaking southern France and spreading rapidly. The creed became known as the *Firmiter credimus*. The particular heretical beliefs that were being fought were based on a posited dichotomy between physical and spiritual: the physical was evil, and the spiritual was good, and human beings are just spiritual beings trapped in physical bodies.

Furthermore, it was forbidden to preach without the approval of the local bishop, and a "master of theology" would be responsible for teaching priesthood candidates in each diocese. These measures were intended to combat the spread of heresy by regulating preaching and religious instruction, to help ensure orthodoxy in teaching.

The council also required the faithful who have reached the age of reason to go to confession at least once a year and to receive Holy Communion at least once a year, preferably during the Easter season. The fathers also sanctioned the use of the term *transubstantiation* to describe what happens at the confecting of the Eucharist, where the substance of the bread and wine completely changes but the accidents (sensory appearances) remain the same.

The Fourth Lateran Council developed the Church's

sacramental theology, defining seven sacraments and explaining that they are visible signs of an invisible reality and the primary means of God communicating his grace to us.

The council also produced constitutions on reform of the Church in discipline, the morality of clerics, the selection of bishops, tithes, simony, and more.

58. What prompted the First Council of Lyons, and what happened?

The First Council of Lyons was held in A.D. 1245 and was convoked and presided over by Pope Innocent IV. This council had much lower attendance than those at the Lateran: it was attended by the Patriarchs of Constantinople, Antioch, and Aquileia (Venice), as well as 140 bishops, Emperor of the East Baldwin II, and Saint Louis, the King of France.

Throughout the Middle Ages, the papacy grew in its temporal power and influence, which increasingly put it at odds with the secular rulers, especially the emperor. This conflict came to a head under Pope Innocent IV (r. 1243–1254) and Emperor Frederick II (r. 1220–1250).

Pope Gregory IX (r. 1227–1241) had tried to resolve the tension with a council in 1240, but Frederick II prevented the meeting with an armed resistance. When Innocent became pope, he pursued Gregory's council agenda himself and, in 1244, convened this council in Lyons. The emperor did not have direct authority there, which allowed for more freedom.

The stated purpose of the council was to ensure that

the Church maintain her proper position in ecclesiastical and temporal matters; to address the strife in the Holy Land; to address the attacks on the Church by the Tatars and others who persecuted and attacked the Church; and specifically to resolve the conflict with the emperor.

From the very start, this was referred to as a general council. Around 140 to 150 bishops were in attendance, because many of Europe's bishops were prevented from being there by Frederick (particularly those in Sicily and Germany), and many in the East were prevented by the Tatars and the Saracen Muslims. As a result, the bishops primarily represented France, Spain, England, and Italy.

The chief act of this council was to depose Emperor Frederick in July 1245, by way of a scathing indictment issued by the council. The fathers also issued some laws pertaining to usury, the Tatars, and the Latin East, but no Church reform canons or condemnations were issued by the council.

59. What prompted the Second Council of Lyons, and what happened?

The Second Council of Lyons was held in A.D. 1274, under Pope Gregory X (r. 1271–1276). There were around 500 bishops in attendance, including fifteen cardinals, as well as the Patriarchs of Constantinople and Antioch, two of the most prominent and significant of the Eastern patriarchates. The presence of these patriarchs is particularly significant considering the schism that went into effect in A.D. 1054 and the mutual excommunications that had been enacted. At this council, what would turn out to be a short-lived reunion of East and West was achieved.

As has so often been the case, this reunification and decision to cooperate came out of the need for a political and/or military alliance. The Byzantine Emperor Michael VIII Paleologus wanted to unite with the pope against Charles of Anjou. However, this reunification was deeply unpopular, and Michael VIII's successor, Andronicus II, nullified it just eight years later in 1282.

There are also records that indicate more than a thousand other invitees were in attendance—dignitaries, theologians, and more. Saint Thomas Aquinas was en route to the council in 1274, and would have been one of these prominent non-council father theologians in attendance, when he died on March 7.

On November 29, 1268, Pope Clement IV (r. 1265–1268) died. The interregnum ("between reigns" of popes) period was incredible and noteworthy, because it lasted nearly *three years*. His successor, Pope Gregory X, was finally elected on September 1, 1271.

This period in Church history was marked by a struggle in which the popes were engaged with the secular authorities, particularly the emperors. The question was what sort of autonomy and unique authority the popes had, over and apart from the emperors. In this light, the emperor Michael VIII Paleologus was in a bitter feud with the popes.

Gregory X wanted to assert the pope's autonomy and exert his own influence over world affairs. He also desired unity between the Eastern and Western churches, a unity that had been broken during the schism of 1054. He wanted to enter into a treaty with Michael VIII Paleologus in the hopes of achieving such a reunion. This would bring peace as well as strength to the Church, which would allow for the pope to exert his authority to end the conflict over the Holy Land.

Pope Gregory called a council, which opened in Lyons on May 7, 1274. There were three priorities: union between East and West; a crusade in the Holy Land; reform of the Church, particularly ethical reform. As we have seen, in the Middle Ages it had become standard for an ecumenical council to spend a great deal of time and effort addressing Church reform—more than simply a tradition, this effort was desperately needed.

The council was attended by around 300 bishops, 60 abbots, and many other clergy and theologians, as well as some secular rulers or their delegates. This is not a particularly large number of attendees, but the makeup of the attendees was ecumenical and universal, representing just about all of Christendom in one form or another.

The union between East and West was achieved at the council, largely through a dogmatic constitution that was issued that dealt with the question of the procession of the Holy Spirit. This was a major point of disagreement between East and West, so the common statement was an opportunity for healing. However, this reunion was very short-lived. Michael VIII Paleologus had imposed the reunion on the East. It is not totally clear why the reunion did not last, although it likely had to do with the fact that the clergy in the East consistently and strongly resisted it, as well as the fact that Gregory's successors would not have the same approach to the matter as he did.

Through the council, a crusade was also planned, and taxes to support it were levied, but the crusade did not come to fruition.

As for the Church reforms, they were not nearly as extensive as Gregory would have liked. But one thing that was accomplished was the establishment of conclaves for papal election. The word conclave comes from the Latin *con clave*, "with a key", referring to the fact that the cardinals would essentially be locked up until a new pope was elected. The three-year interregnum made the need for such an election method quite clear.

60. What prompted the Council of Vienne, and what happened?

The Council of Vienne was held from A.D. 1311–1313 in Vienne, France. This council was attended by around 300 bishops (although the precise number is hard to pin down, as some sources say there were as few as 114), including the Patriarchs of Antioch and Alexandria, as well as three kings—Philip IV of France, Edward II of England, and James II of Aragon.

Pope Clement V (r. 1305–1314) wrote the bull that called the council in Poitiers (France) in 1308. After his election, Clement resided in France, and a few years after his election, he informed the cardinals that he was relocating the papacy to Avignon, in deference to a demand of King Philip IV of France.

Philip IV had had a bitter feud with one of Clement's predecessors, Boniface VIII (r. 1294–1303). Boniface had asserted the papacy's autonomy, and Philip had disagreed and refused to comply; Boniface had threatened him with excommunication, so Philip's thugs had assaulted the pope, who died shortly thereafter. Philip then maintained a certain amount of influence-through-threat over the papacy, and Clement V was in many ways right under Philip's thumb.

However, when Clement decided to call this council, one of the reasons Vienne was chosen as the site was that this was *not* under Philip's jurisdiction.

The council began in October 1311, and Clement outlined the priorities of the council during his opening sermon: the controversy over the Knights Templar; the conflict in the Holy Land; and reform of the Church.

The issue of the Knights Templar was a contentious one; information and accusations were being compiled from across the continent, which delayed the council's work on that matter. Ultimately, Clement decided to suppress the Templars and put all of their massive property and wealth under the control of several other military orders. This appears to have been the result of some behind-the-scenes dealing with Philip and without consulting the council fathers.

It is interesting to note the mode of daily operations at the Council of Vienne, as it is quite different from other councils. Rather than plenary sessions wherein the council fathers all meet and discuss various issues, this council featured a few smaller working groups who would then present their work to the fathers. There was a group of cardinals together with the pope, on the one hand, and a committee that the council fathers elected, on the other. There was also a commission of cardinals that assessed and did the bulk of the work regarding reform of the Church. These groups would then bring their work to the full assembly of fathers, who would confirm the decrees and promulgate them.

61. What prompted the Council of Constance, and what happened?

The Council of Constance was held from A.D. 1414 to 1418, during the Great Schism of the West. Initially convoked illegitimately, the Holy Father would later ratify and approve the council's later sessions.

The object of this council was to end the schism and the great divisions that had arisen in the Church as a result.

At the time of the Council of Constance, there were three rival claimants to the papacy. The (non-ecumenical) council held at Pisa in 1409 had elected Alexander V in an attempt to heal the schism, but this only made the problem worse since the other claimants remained in place. Gregory XII (r. 1406–1415) was the legitimate pope; Benedict XIII was in Avignon; and after Alexander V died, John XXIII was elected to replace him.[5] As we will see, Benedict and John were deposed by the Council of Constance, and Gregory voluntarily resigned in order to allow for a clean slate and a fresh election of a new pontiff.

For some background on the schism, we must discuss the so-called "Avignon papacy", which began in the early fourteenth century, when Pope Clement V moved the papacy from Rome to Avignon. Seventy years later, Saint Catherine of Siena allegedly influenced the pope (Gregory XI) to return to Rome, but by this time a chasm had opened up in the Church's hierarchy. Several cardinals who had become loyal to the Avignon papacy claimed to

[5] The papal names Alexander V, Benedict XIII, and John XXIII, used by fifteenth-century antipopes would all be used later by legitimate popes.

invalidate the election of Pope Urban VI (r. 1378–1389) and "elected" a "pope" of their own. This would not be resolved until the Council of Constance.

Three primary priorities were identified: the eradication of heresy, particularly the heresies espoused by John Wyclif and Jan Hus; the moral reform of the Church; and, most urgently, bringing an end to the schism that had roiled the Church.

The council was initially called by Sigismund (who would later be Holy Roman Emperor), who desperately desired unity for practical reasons: to defend against the invading Turks. Gregory XII, the legitimate pope, later approved of this, and his successor would officially promulgate certain decrees, essentially making *portions* of this council ecumenical.

There is a particular stain on the council's reputation, in spite of its success in healing the schism. Jan Hus, the heretic from Bohemia, was invited to the council and promised safe passage there so that he could face the fathers and try to defend his propositions, but upon his arrival he was executed.

62. What prompted the Council of Basel/Ferrara/Florence, and what happened?

The Council of Basel/Ferrara/Florence (often just called the Council of Florence) was held from A.D. 1431 to 1449. The timeline of this council is complicated and can be a bit confusing, so let's carefully walk through it.

The council first met in Basel, under Pope Eugene IV (r. 1431–1447) and Sigismund, Emperor of the Holy Roman Empire. The goal of this council was to address the heresies cropping up in Bohemia under the followers of Jan Hus. The council's meetings moved from Basel to Ferrara in 1438 and then again to Florence in 1439.

The council first met in Basel beginning in 1431 and was immediately a battleground between the conciliarists and the pope. Pope Eugenius IV ordered that the council should be moved to another city, but the council fathers (the few in attendance) fought back, asserting their own authority even over the pope. The pope even briefly dissolved the council, although before long he was convinced to withdraw that dissolution, and the council's work continued. By 1436, however, there were only twenty bishops in attendance.

In negotiating a meeting with the Eastern churches, the council suggested Avignon, but the city of Ferrara in Italy was selected by the pope and Eastern envoys. The delegation was seven-hundred-strong and included the emperor himself. Work began here in 1438, and in 1439 it again moved to Florence. Here a short-lived reunion between the Eastern and Western churches was negotiated. The Eastern Roman Emperor John VIII (r. 1425–1448) wanted the reunion, as he desired military assistance from the Christian West in the face of attacks by the Ottoman Turks. He sent envoys to the council to try to attain reconciliation, and on July 6, 1439, Pope Eugene IV declared that the Eastern and Western churches were reunited.

In 1453 the Eastern Roman Empire came to an end, however, when the Ottomans captured the capital of Constantinople, which brought the ecclesiastical reunion (which had been quite unpopular in the East) to an end.

While this reunion was being worked out, however, the bishops in Basel were struggling to assert their authority over the pope and even attempted to depose Eugenius and install an anti-pope, Felix V. This anti-pope was accepted by very few, and even those who accepted him renewed their loyalty to Eugenius shortly before his death in 1447. His legitimate successor, Nicholas V (r. 1447–1455), resolved the tension, dissolved the council in 1449, and effectively brought an end to the conflict between the conciliarists and the papacy.

The in-fighting of this period is unfortunate, as various strands of heretical thought were continuing to take over in Europe and the moral rot that was present throughout the Church was taking hold in a more serious way.

63. What prompted the Fifth Lateran Council, and what happened?

The Fifth Lateran Council was held from A.D. 1512 to 1517, under Popes Julius II (r. 1503–1513) and Leo X (r. 1513–1521) and Emperor Maximilian I. It was attended by fifteen cardinals and about eighty archbishops and bishops.

The decrees of the council were primarily disciplinary in nature—they concerned matters of discipline rather than controverted doctrinal topics. The council also indicated a new crusade against the Turks, but the coming of the Reformation in Europe threw these plans into disarray.

The first thing about this council that should leap out at

the student of Church history is the end date: 1517. This is typically recognized as the beginning of the Protestant Reformation, as Martin Luther allegedly nailed his "Ninety-Five Theses" to the door of the Wittenberg Cathedral on October 31 of that year. The need for various types of reform in the Church was widely recognized, and the Fifth Lateran Council was the first serious attempt in any official capacity to achieve these reforms.

The circumstances in which the council was convened tell us a lot about the institutional problems that existed in the Church at the time, which also speaks to *why* reforms were needed, *what* reforms were needed, and *why they didn't happen*. A group of cardinals, with support from the royal houses in Germany and France, called a council to meet in Pisa; in the view of the conciliarists—those who believed an ecumenical council was the ultimate authority in the Church, even above the pope—they had every right to do this. The conciliarists had been able to make inroads in their influence during the preceding centuries because many of the popes were more interested in temporal and secular power and did not concern themselves much with ecclesiastical matters.

However, in response to this, Pope Julius II—a proponent of papal power, both spiritual and temporal (and by no means a reform-minded individual)—called the Fifth Lateran Council to meet in Rome in 1512. In 1513, he was succeeded by Pope Leo X, who continued the work of the council.

The need for reform was widely recognized. As we have seen, this was a standard priority for medieval and renaissance councils. The Fifth Lateran Council was no exception, but the council's efforts toward reform were held up by internal issues, including the remarkably small number of bishops in attendance and Leo's apparent lack of interest in actually carrying the reforms through.

The council's priorities were threefold: brokering peace among the Christian rulers of Europe; reforming the Church where needed; and defending the faith and fighting heresy. The decrees were issued as bulls and explicitly invoked the authority of the bishops meeting in an ecumenical council, presided over by the pope.

In addition, the council approved and promulgated decrees regarding the immortality of the soul, the dignity of bishops, a requirement for clerics' philosophy courses to promote the Christian point of view, and a requirement for the local bishop to grant approval for the printing of books in his territory.

The council's decrees were tremendously ineffective. The widely acknowledged need for Church reform was not met, and the effects of that failure would soon reverberate around the world.

64. What prompted the Council of Trent, and what happened?

The Council of Trent was the nineteenth ecumenical council and was held from A.D. 1545 to 1563. This consisted of twenty-five different sessions; the bishops were not meeting continually for that entire eighteen-year period. The extreme length of this council meant that it spanned *five* popes (Paul III [r. 1534–1549], Julius III [r. 1550–1555], Marcellus II [r. 1555], Paul IV [r. 1555–

1559], and Pius IV [r. 1559–1565]) (although Marcellus II and Paul IV did not convoke any sessions), as well as two emperors (Charles V and Ferdinand). Of course, as we have seen, this means that at the death of each pope, the council officially halted until a successor was elected and he chose to reconvene the council. The council was held in Trent, which is in northern Italy. As was said previously, one of the reasons Trent was chosen as the location was that it would be easy for German Protestants to reach—although no Protestants ended up attending.

The course of Christianity in Europe may have looked very different. When Pope Adrian VI was elected in 1522, he and Emperor Charles V were expected by some to undertake significant Church reforms. But when Adrian died in 1523, his successor, Clement VII (r. 1523–1534), focused his efforts on power struggles in Italy and left the Church's reform on the back burner.

To understand why Church reform had not been accomplished by the various councils, we must remember the power struggle between the conciliarists and the papacy. Because of the tendency to overemphasize the authority of the ecumenical council, popes were reluctant to follow through with even the modest reforms councils enacted. In a sense, it was this problematic power struggle that necessitated Church reform and that made such reform nearly impossible.

There were five cardinal legates of the Holy See, three patriarchs, thirty-three archbishops, 235 bishops, seven abbots, seven generals of monastic orders, and 160 "doctors of divinity" in attendance at the council. They all convened over those eighteen years to confront the greatest challenge the Church had yet faced: the Protestant Reformation. Martin Luther, John Calvin, Ulrich Zwingli, and others had been leading a tidal wave of theological error that was tearing Europe apart and ripping the Church in two. The theological errors espoused by these men were spreading rapidly, and the Church had thus far failed adequately to address them or many of the underlying problems in the Church that helped give rise to the errors and their acceptance by so many Catholics.

In many ways, the Council of Trent was the most superlative council to date. It was the longest; it also issued the most decrees, both on doctrinal and disciplinary matters, of any council up to that date.

The twenty-five sessions of the council were spread out over three general meetings, which were convoked by three popes: Paul III, Julius III, and Pius IV. The first long break in the council's proceedings began in 1547 due to a plague outbreak. The second break began in 1552, because a Lutheran army had amassed near Trent, which threatened the council and fathers. The first meeting addressed such issues as Scripture, justification, and the sacraments of baptism and confirmation, the Catholic teaching concerning which had been challenged in some way or another by the Protestant reformers. There were also disciplinary decrees, reforming the Church's practice regarding the role of bishops in their dioceses.

Paul III died during this plague-induced hiatus, and Julius III was elected as his successor. He reconvened the council in 1551, but, as we have seen, the work of the council was again halted, this time due to the nearby Lutheran army. In this brief period of work, however, decrees on the sacraments of reconciliation, anointing of the sick, and the Eucharist were developed and approved. The council would not meet again for ten years, during which time Julius III and two more popes would die.

Pope Pius IV came to the papacy in 1562, at which point he reconvened the council, which would continue its work until 1563, producing decrees on the Church hierarchy, purgatory, the communion of saints, relics, indulgences, and more. It is clear from this list of topics that the council's work continued to be focused on responding to the errors of Protestantism.

The bishops were the subject of many disciplinary measures passed by the council. This is fitting, because the moral failings of bishops had led to much suffering in the preceding centuries, and no previous council had succeeded in reforming the episcopacy. Bishops were now required to live within their diocese, and, in the event they had to leave the diocese, they had to return within three months; they were also required to preach every Sunday and to visit every parish in their diocese at least once a year; other canons were passed, all of which would have a tremendous effect on the holiness and practical effectiveness of the episcopal ministry.

Many practical abuses were addressed by the council. One of these was the appointment of laymen as bishops; this often led to these young men simply collecting the payment of a bishop without ever being ordained a priest, let alone serving as bishop of his see. One of the most fundamental and important actions of the Council of Trent pertained to the education of clerics. Essentially, many priests were apprenticed and not given a systematic theological or practical education, which meant that a great many priests were insufficiently prepared for ministry. The council mandated a seminary for each diocese, where priestly formation (spiritual and intellectual) could be regularized and monitored. This reform would allow diocesan clergy around the world to achieve the standard that had been set by their religious order counterparts, who were quite well-trained in their monasteries. While the seminary system is by no means perfect, this reform may have had the most significant and far-reaching positive consequences of any reform to come out of the Council of Trent.

Sacred Scripture was addressed by the council as well. The Protestant reformers had chosen not to recognize seven books from the Old Testament (Tobit, Judith, Wisdom, Sirach, and 1 Maccabees as well as additions to Esther and Daniel) as inspired. The council affirmed the ancient belief, which had been previously codified at local councils, that these books were indeed canonical and that Scripture must be interpreted in conformity with the teaching of the Church. In addition, Sacred Tradition was recognized as an authoritative source of truth, protected by the Holy Spirit like all magisterial teaching.

The theology and pastoral legitimacy of indulgences were affirmed by the council, but the fathers also made clear that they should in no way be bought or sold. This, of course, had been the spark that lit the powder keg of the Reformation decades earlier.

In light of the great amount of doctrinal confusion that was spreading, the council also produced a universal catechism, commonly known as the *Catechism of the Coun-*

cil of Trent. This would be the primary tool for teaching the faith (and for developing local catechisms) until the development of the *Catechism of the Catholic Church* at the end of the twentieth century.

One of Trent's most widely recognized reforms had to do with the Sacred Liturgy. The wide variety in liturgical practices was largely suppressed—although we must be careful not to exaggerate this point. A certain amount of liturgical variety was maintained, but by and large the liturgy would now be uniformly celebrated around the world. This would be regulated by a new congregation in the Roman Curia. The missal published in the wake of the Council of Trent would, by and large, remain unaltered until the Second Vatican Council.

After a long, contentious, and even dangerous council, many of the bishops would have been happy to publish the decrees and move on. But true reformers (such as Saint Charles Borromeo), who recognized the dangerous state the Church was in, immediately began the work of implementing the council's teachings. The Church was unified in purpose, and the pope and many of the bishops were invigorated with a fervor that had not been seen in a long time. The problems in discipline and application of doctrine that had resulted in the Protestant Reformation were addressed in no uncertain terms. While it was too late to stop the schism, the efforts of these many saintly men and women certainly stopped the bleeding, so to speak, and allowed the Church to become stronger than ever.

65. Why was there such a long time between the Council of Trent and the First Vatican Council, with no other councils?

Briefly, there was no identified need for a council during that time. Councils do not happen at regular intervals and are only convened when there is a pressing need that must be addressed by the universal Church, specifically by all the bishops in union with the pope. If no such need is identified, no ecumenical council will be called.

66. What prompted the First Vatican Council, and what happened?

The First Vatican Council was held in A.D. 1869–1870, convoked by Blessed Pope Pius IX (r. 1846–1878). It was convoked by the bull *Aeterni Patris* (not to be confused with the 1879 encyclical of the same name by Pope Leo XIII) on June 29, 1868.

In this bull, Pius IX explains the authority of the supreme pontiff, as the successor of Saint Peter, to call ecumenical councils in order to meet the needs of the Church and respond to some danger or threat that the Church faces, as well as to fulfill his normal obligation to do so. He identified a number of threats to faith and morals that the Church needed to act quickly to combat.

The two primary aims of this council were to condemn errors that were poisoning the hearts and minds of the faithful and solemnly to define Catholic teaching on certain aspects of the Church. Pius had been fighting modern heresy for his entire papacy, and this council was a sort of culmination of that fight.

The council ran from December 8, 1869, to July 18, 1870. In attendance were six archbishop-princes, forty-nine cardinals, eleven patriarchs, 680 archbishops and bishops, twenty-eight abbots, and twenty-nine generals of orders. The Eastern Orthodox churches were invited to send observers, and they took great offense at such an invitation, and no observers were sent.

Ultimately, in the short time the council fathers met (just three sessions over the course of seven months), they discussed and approved two constitutions: the Dogmatic Constitution on the Catholic Faith (*Dei Filius*), and the First Dogmatic Constitution on the Church of Christ (*Pastor Aeternus*, which, among other things, dealt with the questions of primacy, teaching authority, and papal infallibility).

The culmination of Pius' fight against the modernists' errors was in *Dei Filius*, which aimed to outline and defend truths of the faith against modernism, including a clear statement that faith and reason go hand in hand, that we can know God and discover the truth through our God-given gift of reason (apart from those truths that can only be known through revelation). This was a clear and explicit repudiation of the anti-religious Enlightenment ideals.

This council is best known for its definition of papal infallibility. (See question 69.) This was a point of some controversy among the bishops; some did not think it was the right time to define—and thus highlight—this teaching. But in the end, of course, the definition was included in *Pastor Aeternus*. The council fathers intended to undertake a great deal more work, and further documents would have also included elaboration of the teaching authority of councils, bishops, etc. But the council was cut short, and the fathers' work was left uncompleted.

More than a few bishops did not think it an opportune time to define papal infallibility, as they thought it would cause strife and division in the Church and not necessarily even be understood. Nearly a hundred bishops initially voted against including the definition; by the time the final vote rolled around, those still opposed had decided to abstain from voting rather than voting against it (with the exception of two bishops who apparently did not get that message).

It is important to note that the bishops who voted against the definition of infallibility were not necessarily opposed to the doctrine itself—the doctrine is an ancient one, going all the way back to Christ's promise that the gates of hell would not prevail against the Church (see Mt 16:18). Rather, they were opposed to the definition being included in *Pastor Aeternus*. They had various reasons for their hesitancy: some thought it would cause issues with secular authorities; some thought it would cause ecumenical problems with the Orthodox; some worried that the teaching would be misunderstood by Catholics and result in internal problems within the Church. But ultimately, of course, the definition was included in the document.

The council was suddenly and unexpectedly halted, and much of its work was left uncompleted.

67. Why was the First Vatican Council left uncompleted?

In 1870, the Franco-Prussian War broke out on the European continent, and this war's progression would have a profound effect on Italy. The Papal States, which up to that point had been significant tracts of land in central Italy governed by the pope, would cease to be as a result of this war and would be subsumed into the newly unified Italian state. (The Vatican would not regain autonomy until the Lateran Treaty of 1929.)

On September 10, 1870, Italy declared war on the Papal States, and troops began to surge into the territories. The bishops had been allowed to leave Rome and return to their home dioceses as these tensions escalated.

The council was indefinitely adjourned on October 20, 1870, after Piedmontese troops entered Rome; it never resumed. In fact, it was not formally closed, either, until just before the Second Vatican Council, when Church authorities realized a new council could not really be convened until the previous one had closed.

Only a small fraction of the work that was intended for the council was completed.

68. Are its decrees still valid, even though it ended under such strange circumstances?

Yes. A council's being unexpectedly interrupted does not suddenly render it ineffectual or optional. Because the pope was present and presided over the council's work, the decrees were published as "bulls", specifically declaring the council's authority. In other words, as the council's work progressed, the decrees were published authoritatively.

69. So what exactly is "papal infallibility"?

When we want to understand papal infallibility, we must recognize what it is *not*. Papal infallibility does not mean that the pope is sinless or impeccable; it does not mean that he always tells the truth; it does not mean that he receives new prophecies or divine inspiration or new revelation. It does not mean that the pope will necessarily understand the Catholic faith better than others. Throughout history, many popes have made many mistakes, and all have been sinners.

Papal infallibility is an insurance policy. It is a protection, something to keep the Church safe from error. Jesus promised to send the paraclete, the helper, the Holy Spirit (cf. Jn 14:15–27) and that the gates of hell would not prevail against the Church (see Mt 16:18). Here is how the First Vatican Council defined papal infallibility in *Pastor Aeternus*:

> Therefore, faithfully adhering to the tradition received from the beginning of the Christian faith, to the glory of God our savior, for the exaltation of the Catholic religion and for the salvation of the Christian people, with the approval of the Sacred Council, we teach and define as a divinely revealed dogma that when the Roman Pontiff speaks EX CATHEDRA, that is, when, in the exercise of his office as shepherd and teacher of all Christians, in virtue of his supreme apostolic authority, he defines a doctrine concerning faith or morals to be held by the whole Church, he possesses, by the divine assistance promised to him in blessed Peter, that infallibility which the divine Redeemer willed his Church to enjoy in defining doctrine concerning faith or morals. Therefore, such definitions of the Roman Pontiff are of themselves, and not by the consent of the Church, irreformable. (*Pastor Aeternus* 9)

It does not matter who the pope is, what he knows, how holy or wicked he might be personally—the Holy Spirit protects the Church from error in her definitive teachings. It is important to understand that infallibility in teaching is limited to matters pertaining to faith and morals, presented as things to be held definitively by all the faithful.

70. What prompted the Second Vatican Council, and what happened?

The Second Vatican Council was held from A.D. 1962 to 1965, called by Pope Saint John XXIII (r. 1958–1963) and continued under his successor, Pope Saint Paul VI (r. 1963–1978). The primary purpose of this council was to present the teachings of the Church for modern man. It addressed relations between the Church and the modern world, as well as the Church's relationship with other Christians and non-Christians, and the Church's relationship with herself. It was the second council to be held at Saint Peter's Basilica.

The council ultimately issued sixteen documents, some on internal ecclesiastical issues, and some on how the Church relates to the rest of the world. While, of course, the council reiterated and defended the deposit of faith and the Church's ancient teaching, ecclesiastical life would change in some very noticeable ways in the council's aftermath.

The exact circumstances that prompted Pope John to call the council are not clear. He must have known he was not long for this world, as he was already seventy-six years old and in poor health. But he quickly decided to convene the council, announcing that the council would aim to renew the spirit of the Gospel in the hearts of people everywhere and to adjust Christian discipline to modern-day living.

The council was attended by some 2,500 bishops from all over the world, as well as 150 superiors of religious orders. In addition, there were official observers, including Orthodox and Protestant, as well as theological advisors for the council fathers, known as *periti*.

Pope Pius XII (r. 1939–1958) had spoken of a need for an ecumenical council, but his papacy ended before such a council could be summoned. (There was also not much support in the hierarchy for such a move.) As his successor, the cardinals selected the elderly patriarch of Venice, Angelo Cardinal Roncalli, who would take the name John XXIII. Less than three months after his election, he announced the Second Vatican Council, which would begin a few years later.

While some saw the council as unnecessary, there were also those who saw a need for more lay participation in Church life, a new examination of the Church's relationship with non-Catholics and even non-Christians, Roman curial reform, and many issues with the way the Church engages and interacts with the modern world. So the goal of the council was to prepare and equip the Church for such engagement. It was about presenting the Church's timeless teaching in a way that the modern world as a whole, and individuals, could engage with.

When John XXIII died in 1963, shortly after the first session of the council concluded, the council's continuation was by no means a foregone conclusion. A great debate ensued, until his successor, Saint Paul VI, decided that the council would continue its work.

Several documents the council produced emphasized the important role of the laity in the Church's evangelizing work, especially *Apostolicam actuositatem* (the Decree on the Apostolate of the Laity), *Lumen Gentium* (the Dogmatic Constitution on the Church), which insisted on that universal call to holiness and the role of the laity in evangelizing in all walks of life, as well as *Gaudium et Spes* (the Pastoral Constitution on the Church in the Modern World). Catholics are not to separate their faith from the rest of their lives, but are to live them united, with their faith informing and influencing every aspect of their lives.

The universal call to holiness among all the faithful—clergy as well as laity—is one of the primary fruits of the council. As we have seen, just about every ecumenical council since the Middle Ages included attempts at reforming the Church and enacting disciplinary canons. The universal call to holiness of the Second Vatican Council is another attempt to call everyone to that saintly state and evangelizing mission.

The council also emphasized the important teaching and authoritative role of each individual bishop and the college of bishops corporately, in *Lumen Gentium*. Rather than a neo-conciliarist viewpoint, this was simply a recapturing of the ancient understanding of the bishop as head of the Church in his territory.

One of the greatest misunderstandings of the council's work would be the alleged removal of Latin from the Mass and what sometimes almost seemed to be a mandate to use only the *vernacular*, the language spoken by the local congregation. On the contrary, the council allowed for the vernacular in certain circumstances and in certain parts of the (Latin) liturgy, and in the years that would follow, while emphasizing the importance of retaining Latin, this permission for some use of the vernacular was taken well beyond the stated will of the council fathers.

Protestant and Orthodox observers attended the council on invitation, which was an important ecumenical gesture. They were observers and did not have a vote or any role in constructing the council's documents.

The decree on religious liberty, *Dignitatis Humanae* (Human Dignity), was one of the least popular documents among the council fathers and had the most votes against it—although it is important to note that it was still not very many! It remains one of the most controversial points of the council's work. In effect, this document served as a reminder that even those in error must be treated with respect and reiterated that coercion in matters of faith and religious practice is not appropriate —coercion is not the same as conversion.

The council (particularly in the Dogmatic Constitution on Divine Revelation, *Dei Verbum*) also encouraged Catholics to study the Bible while reiterating that the Bible must be read with the eyes and guidance of the Church. The practice of a permanent diaconate was restored, a practice that has subsequently borne great fruit in many places around the world.

The Second Vatican Council took place during a time of unprecedented media access—the media had unprecedented access to the council, and people around the world had unprecedented access to the media. Every day, newspapers and television programs would report on the council's work, the debates, any interesting developments. For the first time, an ecumenical council was a worldwide sensation.

It is interesting to note that four men who participated in the first session of the council later became pope: Cardinal Giovanni Battista Montini (Saint Paul VI); Bishop Albino Luciani (John Paul I); Bishop Karol Wojtyła (Saint John Paul II); Father Joseph Ratzinger, (as a theological consultant, or *peritus* [Benedict XVI]).

The years and decades since the council's end have been rough, to say the least. Seminary enrollment and ordinations have plummeted; the number of professed men and women religious has likewise taken a huge hit; many Catholic schools have (explicitly or implicitly) abandoned their Catholic identity; faith formation is in tatters in many places. But there are tremendous signs of hope, as well, and more and more as the years go by.

The Second Vatican Council remains relatively recent, and so it is difficult to assess its ultimate legacy. It is easy to see the legacy of the First Council of Nicaea or the Council of Chalcedon. But the Second Vatican Council is too fresh, too much of a battleground, for us really to understand its legacy.

71. *What is ressourcement? What is aggiornamento?*

Ressourcement is a French term that refers to a "return to the sources". In the context of the Second Vatican

Council, this meant a return to and rediscovery of the authoritative sources of Christianity, including Sacred Scripture and the Church Fathers. The idea was that if we went back to the fundamentals to rediscover the foundations of the faith, we could revitalize our evangelistic efforts in the context of the modern world. This idea also manifested itself in the efforts of many religious orders to reexamine their roots, their founding, and their early history, in an effort to reinvigorate their work and religious life.

Aggiornamento is an Italian word that means "to bring up to date" or "modernize". While this "modernization" can be a temptation to try to change Church teaching to fit modern sensibilities, it should be interpreted rather as an "appropriate adaptation of Church discipline to the needs and conditions of our times", as Saint John XXIII wrote in *Ad Petri cathedram*, his first encyclical.

72. What is the "Spirit of Vatican II"?

Simply put, the so-called "Spirit of Vatican II" is an interpretation of the council that does not adhere strictly to the documents produced by the council, but rather insists on a reading of the council's objectives and directives that is not explicitly detailed in the documents. Those who espouse the "Spirit of Vatican II" look beyond the texts themselves to support their agenda. Often elements of this agenda are at odds with the council itself.

73. Have any councils ever been overruled, undone, or annulled?

No ecumenical council has been overruled, undone, or annulled in its entirety. As we have seen in our historical walk through each council, some councils have had certain canons not accepted by the pope, and others have had their disciplinary measures overturned at a later date. But no council has been entirely annulled and rejected.

74. Did the twenty-one ecumenical councils all get such recognition right away, or was it in retrospect they were recognized as such?

Most of these councils were immediately identified and acknowledged as ecumenical and authoritative at the time they were held. Although in the early centuries of the Church, the pope was not typically in attendance at the councils, his acceptance of their teaching (and accepting that teaching as his own) came fairly quickly.

As we have seen, in the case of the First Council of Constantinople (A.D. 381), the pope was not involved in the convening or the proceedings of the council—it was a general synod of the East, and only bishops from the Eastern Empire were in attendance. However, the pope was supportive of the council, and after the fact its decrees were ratified and applied to the universal Church. The same thing happened at the Third Council of Constantinople in A.D. 553.

This might seem a bit strange to us, as the pope has

been in attendance for the last several ecumenical councils and has been intimately involved in the councils' convocation, agenda, and even day-to-day operations.

THEOLOGICAL QUESTIONS

75. Can a council override a pope?

No, and this is a question that caused a fair amount of strife in the life of the Church from the fourteenth to sixteenth centuries. As with so many of our questions here, it is fundamentally a matter of authority. One school of thought, called "conciliarism", says that councils are the highest authority in the Church, even over and above the pope. This is an erroneous belief and is contrary to Jesus' placement of Peter as the head of the apostles and granting him unique authority that the other apostles do not have. We can also see, even from the earliest days of the Church, that the primacy of Rome (the See of Peter) was acknowledged in belief and in practice.

Canon law expressly lays out the punishment for anyone trying to use a council to act against a pope: "One who takes recourse against an act of a Roman Pontiff to an ecumenical council or the college of bishops is to be punished with a censure" (can. 1372). This is the current legislation, as contained in the 1983 *Code of Canon Law*.

The Pio-Benedictine Code of 1917 read: "Each and every one of whatever status, grade, or condition, even if he is regal, episcopal, or cardinalatial, appealing from the laws, decrees, or mandates of the Roman Pontiff existing at that time to a Universal Council, is suspected of heresy and by that fact incurs excommunication specially reserved to the Apostolic See" (1917 *CIC* 2332).

76. Can a pope override a council?

Again, to answer this question we must consider the different levels of authority held by different teachings of councils. For example, pastoral pronouncements or instructions proclaimed by a council—such as those from the Second Vatican Council—are not infallible and are not unalterable. In that sense, a pope could certainly later change course from what a council proclaimed. But in doctrinal definitions, as we have seen, ecumenical councils are protected by the charism of infallibility, as is the pope under the proper conditions, so they cannot be at odds. No pope will ever come along and say that Christ is not of the same substance as the Father (First Council of Nicaea), that the substance of the Eucharist does not change while the accidents remain the same (Fourth Lateran Council), or that the pope does not teach infallibly under certain conditions (First Vatican Council). These are dogmatic pronouncements, explanations, made by ecumenical councils, protected by the Holy Spirit from being in error.

77. Do councils always produce documents?

Each council produces something different—it all depends on the context, the purpose of the council, and what sort of document would be the most effective. Sometimes the council simply releases "canons", sometimes bulls, sometimes constitutions or declarations or something else altogether. But there is always something produced and published as a result of the council's work.

The earliest conciliar document we have today is contained in the Acts of the Apostles (cf. Acts 15:23–29). This is a letter that was sent by the Council of Jerusalem to the Christians in Antioch, Syria, and Cilicia about the year A.D. 50.

There are all sorts of what might be called *working documents* that the council uses in its day-to-day proceedings, but these are not considered magisterial conciliar documents when released. These would include speeches, reports, and drafts, and they are called the "acts" of the council. They can be very interesting for those who wish to explore the inner workings of a council or see how certain teachings or formulations developed over the council's course. Sometimes the diaries or memoirs of council fathers will also be published, which—while, of course, not magisterial or official in any way—can give fascinating insights into how a council's work progressed and how the fathers reached their ultimate decisions.

78. Do these different types of documents have different weights of authority?

The documents that are produced by an ecumenical council vary from council to council. In many cases, the council promulgated canons (or rules) or decrees. In the Middle Ages, the council's decisions were often promulgated as papal bulls, giving them instantaneous and clear papal recognition and approval. The Second Vatican Council's documents fell under three primary categories: constitutions, declarations, and decrees, and they were also designated as either dogmatic or pastoral. They are designated as such according to their subject matter, and its depth of treatment.

As for the authority that each document carries, the most important thing to remember is that these documents are produced by ecumenical councils, which means they are intended for the universal Church and represent the teaching of all the bishops in union with the pope. This is the highest teaching authority in the Church; even when a document is not providing new definitions or explanations of dogmas, it still carries that authority. Even a policy or practical matter decreed by an ecumenical council is still given authoritatively. Of course, not every document is of equal weight or importance in the life of the Church, but we should not take this as an excuse to disregard those documents we don't personally like.

79. *I've seen the word "anathema" in regard to councils, as in "let him be anathema." What does "anathema" mean?*

"Anathema" is a Greek term meaning "placed on high", "suspended", or "set aside", sometimes meant as set aside *for destruction*. In the canons of many ecumenical councils, we read that a person or proposition is *anathema*. When Church councils declared someone *anathema*, all it meant was that this person was "set aside" or had broken from communion with the Church. It is not a pronouncement of eternal damnation or anything of the sort—rather, it became a legal term indicating a break in communion.

The term has a rich history, with deep scriptural precedents. In the Old Testament, it was used to refer to offerings made to God and, often, things that were destroyed in this offering. We see the term (its Hebrew equivalent, *kherem*) referring to objects (Deut 7:26, 13:17), people (1 Kings 20:42, Is 34:5), land (Lev 27:21, Zech 14:11), and more. In some cases, these *kherem* were hung in the temple in order to be visible (suspended, set aside, placed on high), but sometimes the term was used for something that was set aside because it was cursed and had to be avoided. In the New Testament, we see the Greek term *anathema* used in the sense of a curse for those who deny and reject the gospel (Gal 1:8–9) or separate themselves from the Body of Christ in some other way (Rom 9:6). In several places, Saint Paul uses the term *anathema* in the same context in which it is used in council decrees, for example: "If anyone has no love for the Lord, let him be accursed [*anathema*]" (1 Cor 16:22). This anathematizing has one goal: to prompt repentance and reconciliation in the excommunicated. (There is much, much more that could be said about this term, its usage, and its formal application in Church law, but the present volume does not allow for such a detailed explanation.)

It should be noted that *anathematization* no longer exists as a formal penalty in ecclesiastical law, as it was removed in the 1983 *Code of Canon Law*.

80. How can it be said that the pope is teaching in union with all the bishops when (a) not all validly ordained bishops attend, (b) some of them vote against certain measures, and (c) some of them explicitly teach something different?

This is a very thorny question, and one that has caused a great deal of disagreement and tension between the Orthodox and Catholics over the centuries. As we've seen, the last ecumenical council to be held in the East was the Fourth Council of Constantinople in A.D. 869–870. After that, it was extremely rare for Eastern bishops to participate in ecumenical councils. Once the Catholic Church and Orthodox split from each other, the Orthodox definitively stopped attending ecumenical councils. Furthermore, there are (unfortunately) a great number of validly ordained bishops who are in personal schism or some other irregular situation; bishops might be ill or otherwise unable to attend the council; some bishops vote against certain measures that become the council's official teaching; and some validly ordained bishops fall into heresy and explicitly try to teach contrary to what the council teaches. So how can it be said that "all the bishops" are teaching in union with the pope?

We shouldn't think of "all the bishops teaching in unison" as every single validly (whether licitly or not) ordained bishop in the world, and of there being zero disagreement among them.

As to bishops who are separated from the Church, it all comes down to whether or not the bishop is in communion with Rome. In order to be considered part of the college of bishops, a man must be validly ordained *and* in communion with the pope. Ontologically, the man remains a bishop forever due to the indelible mark left by the sacrament of Holy Orders. But if a bishop is not in communion with Rome, then he is not a part of the college of bishops.

In the case of bishops who are *unable* to attend or who vote against a particular document or proposition or definition: the bishops present at a council agree to operate under the typical terms of a council, including voting on propositions by those who are able to be present. They do not have to come to a consensus; it is more of a *moral consensus*, rather than a numerical consensus.

81. Do the councils ever contradict each other?

When it comes to definitions on matters of faith and morals, ecumenical councils will never contradict each other. On such issues, these councils teach infallibly, and truth cannot contradict truth. However, as we have seen, councils do not only produce infallible statements and documents, and some concerned themselves explicitly with disciplinary matters, on which the Church can certainly change from time to time. In those contexts, councils have come to some differing conclusions.

There is another example that is occasionally given, from the Council of Constance (1414–1418). As we saw earlier, this council was initially convoked illegitimately and only became legitimate and ecumenical in its final few sessions. The earlier sessions, which were not canonical and thus not binding, indicated that the council had supreme authority, even over and above the pope. This is *conciliarism*, which is explicitly contraindicated by the First Vatican Council, in particular. But because these first sessions were not approved or their decrees promulgated by the pope, they are not part of an ecumenical council, and as a result, in reality there is no contradiction here.

Another example that is often trotted out is that of the Council of Florence. This council declared that a constituent and necessary part of priestly ordination was for the chalice and paten to be given to the man being ordained; this is certainly part of the ordination rite, but Pope Pius XII (nearly 500 years later) declared that this was not a *necessary* part of a valid ordination, but rather the laying on of hands effected the ordination. However, this is not a council being contradicted by later definitive Church teaching; rather, this is simply a liturgical regulation that was changed, which is completely within the purview of the Church to do.

82. *Could a council ever remove a pope?*

No. There are only two ways for a papacy to end: the death of the pope or the pope's free and unprovoked resignation. From time to time, there has been discussion of making some provision for the removal of a pope by a third party—typically an ecumenical council or a super majority of the college of cardinals. But because the pope "enjoys supreme, full, immediate and universal ordinary power in the Church, which he can always freely exercise" (*CIC* 331), there can be no intervention by an outside party. Essentially, the matter is between the pope and God.

83. Since a pope is the one who calls a council, what happens if a pope dies partway through?

This is not a purely hypothetical question—this has happened many times in the Church's history. Most recently, both the Council of Trent and the Second Vatican Council ran through multiple papacies. In the case of Vatican II, Pope Saint John XXIII had called the council, which opened its first session in 1962. He had only been pope for a few years at that point, but felt compelled to call the council for various reasons (see question 70). He died somewhat unexpectedly, which put everything on hold. When the pope dies, *everything* goes on hold except the most fundamental operations of the Holy See. It is up to his successor to decide whether or not to retain cardinals in their positions and any number of other things. In the event that an ecumenical council was underway at the death of the previous pope, his successor must decide what to do.

Pope Saint Paul VI succeeded John in 1963 and decided to reconvene the council. The next session was held from September to December 1963, just about three months after Paul became pope.

The right of the new pope to decide a council's course is enshrined in the *Code of Canon Law*: "If the Apostolic See becomes vacant during the celebration of a council, it is interrupted by the law itself until a new Supreme

Pontiff orders it to be continued or dissolves it" (*CIC* 340).

84. Do synods of bishops have the same infallibility as ecumenical councils?

The question of infallibility as it pertains to synods of bishops boils down to the question of authority: Why is a synod of bishops meeting, and whom are they teaching? As we have seen, the synod of bishops is convened, not as a teaching body, but rather as an advisory body to the pope. As such, deliberations and conversations and discussions would not be protected by the charism of infallibility. This differs from an ecumenical council, in which all the bishops of the world teach in union with the pope, and the Holy Spirit protects them from teaching error.

85. Is a council infallible in its own right, or does it only get that protection when the pope signs off on its decrees? In other words, does infallibility only apply to the successor of Saint Peter, or do the successors to the apostles—teaching in unison— have the same protection, apart from the pope?

The question of infallibility in regard to an ecumenical council is more complex than "is the council infallible". But fundamentally we can rephrase the question in a more helpful way, addressing it to individual teachings of a council, rather than to whole documents or to the entire body of a council's work.

The Holy Spirit protects the pope and the bishops from teaching error in the Church's definitive doctrine and leading the Church and the faithful astray. So we can trust that the Church will not teach error in the context of an ecumenical council, when the pope and all the bishops define Church teaching. Of course, this does not mean that every word pronounced by an ecumenical council is of divine inspiration or even unassailably true. But when defining matters pertaining to faith and morals and invoking the teaching authority granted to them, the council fathers are protected from teaching error. The pope's ratification of those decrees is more like an official stamp of approval rather than a retroactive gift of infallibility.

86. Were there ever any councils at which the pope was not involved?

Yes. In fact, there are two councils now recognized as ecumenical by the Catholic Church at which the pope had no involvement whatsoever: the First Council of Constantinople (A.D. 381) and the Second Council of Constantinople (A.D. 553). As we have seen, the pope did not convoke these councils, nor did he participate in their day-to-day activity. But they are reckoned as ecumenical because the pope later acknowledged them as such and promulgated their decrees.

87. Why do the bishops have special authority when teaching all together, as opposed to teaching individually on their own?

This really boils down to a question of jurisdiction. The local bishop has authority in his territory, but all the bishops of the world teaching *together* in an ecumenical council have universal jurisdiction.

The Second Vatican Council taught that:

> Although the individual bishops do not enjoy the prerogative of infallibility, they nevertheless proclaim Christ's doctrine infallibly whenever, even though dispersed through the world, but still maintaining the bond of communion among themselves and with the successor of Peter, and authentically teaching matters of faith and morals, they are in agreement on one position as definitively to be held. This is even more clearly verified when, gathered together in an ecumenical council, they are teachers and judges of faith and morals for the universal Church, whose definitions must be adhered to with the submission of faith. (*Lumen Gentium* 25)

The individual bishops, although they are the primary teachers of the faith in their territories, do not enjoy infallibility, but as a united teaching body, the bishops corporately do.

CONTROVERSIES

88. Why is Vatican II so controversial?

The Second Vatican Council has been a source of controversy since Saint John XXIII first announced his intention to call an ecumenical council on January 25, 1959.
At the time the council was announced, many did not
see a need for it.

The primary points of controversy came up in the documents the council produced. Nearly all of these contro-
versies, however, arise from a misunderstanding of what
the council taught. There is even a movement that ostensibly aims to discover the *true* meaning of the council's
documents—which, perversely, is nearly always at odds
with the plain meaning of the text.

Fundamentally, however, the council is controversial
because there are those who do not like what it yielded.
This is complicated by the fact that, in many ways, what
the council yielded is not what the council fathers had
in mind. So, many decades later, the twentieth-first ecumenical council remains controversial, remains one of
the chief and most volatile battlegrounds in the life of
the Church.

89. Did Vatican II change the Church's teaching on ecumenism?

This is one of the most common accusations made against the Second Vatican Council, but it has no basis in reality.

The fundamental teaching of Vatican II on ecumenism can be found in *Lumen Gentium*, and this is the lens through which everything else must be read: the document describes those who are in danger as "knowing that the Catholic Church was made necessary by Christ, would refuse either to enter or to remain in it" (*LG* 14). In other words, *outside the Church there is no salvation*. We can unpack this a little bit. As the *Catechism* says: "Reformulated positively, it means that all salvation comes from Christ the Head through the Church which is his Body" (*CCC* 846). This is an incredibly controversial proposition, and much has been made of Vatican II's approach to the question, with many claiming that the council tried to undo this teaching of the Church. But as we can see from this quote from *Lumen Gentium*, this is not the case. What the council did was to articulate the reality that those who knowingly deny the truth of the Catholic faith put their souls in danger; but anyone who is saved is saved through the merits of the Catholic Church.

The Church's approach to non-Catholic Christians is articulated in *Unitatis Redintegratio*, the Council's Decree on Ecumenism, which says, ". . . all who have been justified by faith in Baptism are members of Christ's body" (*Unitatis Redintegratio* 3). As joined to the Body of Christ through baptism, they are united, even if imperfectly, to the Catholic Church. It is a sort of imperfect communion, but communion nonetheless, by virtue of our shared baptism.

90. *What are the arguments people make against Vatican II? In other words, why do some people not accept Vatican II?*

There are some groups that do not accept the teachings of the Second Vatican Council and some groups who only accept *some* of the council's teachings. At the risk of generalizing, most of these groups feel that the council taught innovations, and some make the claim that Vatican II was in effect the founding of a new, schismatic church that split off from the True Church, which is now maintained by a select few. Some even claim that the council bears no authoritative weight, because (they claim) John XXIII was an anti-pope, not a valid successor of Peter, and thus did not have the authority to call a council in the first place, let alone ratify and promulgate its decisions.

While these views sound radical, they are by no means unique. Throughout the Church's history, we have seen many, many instances of groups who did not accept a given council's teaching. This problem persists down to our own day and is no less serious an ecumenical problem. Such an attitude does damage to the Body of Christ, and we must continue to strive to heal those wounds.

*91. Vatican II is often called a "pastoral council",
    as opposed to a "teaching council". Is this a fair
    description/distinction to make? Where does this
    distinction come from?*

Referring to the council as "pastoral" is by no means a
slur. From its beginning, this was the explicit goal and
character of the council. On the opening day of the
council (October 11, 1962), Pope Saint John XXIII gave
an address titled *Gaudet Mater Ecclesia*, in which he said
the council was to be "predominantly pastoral in character". After this, that descriptor was used repeatedly by
the council fathers during their various addresses and re-
marks.

The important thing here is to avoid thinking of a "pastoral council" as any less binding or less serious than a
"doctrinal council". They are simply addressing different
sorts of questions, different types of issues faced by the
Church. But regardless of this distinction, it remains an
ecumenical council.

The pastoral character of the council does not mean
there was no dogmatic teaching; on the contrary, there
was a great deal of dogmatic teaching at Vatican II! While
no definitions of dogma were given, dogmatic teaching
was nevertheless presented by the council. This should
be obvious from the fact that some of the council's documents are titled *dogmatic constitutions*.

It is also interesting to note that Vatican II has been
the most representative of the worldwide Church. For
the first time, due to ease of communications as well
as ease of travel, an ecumenical council was attended by

bishops truly from all over the world, representing the universal Catholic Church. While this does not make the council's decrees any more binding or forceful than those of another council, it does help to emphasize the authority of the council, with the worldwide episcopacy teaching in union with the pope.

One final note: we do not only hear about doctrinal and pastoral councils. The First, Second, and Third Lateran Councils became known as "disciplinary councils" because of the issues they addressed. No doctrinal matters were addressed at these councils, let alone any dogmas defined.

92. Did the Second Vatican Council ban the use of Latin in the Mass and the teaching of Latin in seminaries and Catholic schools?

This is a common misconception about the Second Vatican Council and one that has itself resulted in a great deal of division. The council's *Constitution on the Sacred Liturgy* (*Sacrosanctum Concilium*) actually says the following about Latin in the liturgy: "The use of the Latin language is to be preserved in the Latin rites" (*SC* 36); "Steps should be taken so that the faithful may also be able to say or to sing together in Latin those parts of the Ordinary of the Mass which pertain to them" (*SC* 54); "The Church acknowledges Gregorian chant as specially suited to the Roman liturgy; therefore, other things being equal, it should be given pride of place in liturgical services" (*SC* 116). *Sacrosanctum Concilium* preserved Latin as the primary and official language of the Church.

This was in complete continuity with what came before, including Saint John XXIII's encyclical *Veterum sapientiae* of February 1962, shortly before the council's opening. In this letter, the Holy Father wrote that the Latin language should be maintained or restored as necessary, and its use in the liturgy and in seminary training be encouraged and promoted. He described the use of Latin as "ancient and uninterrupted" and directed that it remain so.

Even following the council, the directives from Rome continued to emphasize the importance of Latin. The 1983 Code of Canon Law states: "The Eucharist is to be celebrated in the Latin language or in another language provided the liturgical texts have been legitimately approved" (*CIC* 928). Saint John Paul II wrote in 2002: "The Roman Church has special obligations towards Latin, the splendid language of ancient Rome, and she must manifest them whenever the occasion presents itself" (*Dominicae cenae* 10).

These are but a few examples, but they demonstrate the Church's continued emphasis on the importance of Latin, particularly in the context of the liturgy.

93. If it is a pastoral council, does that mean its documents are not binding?

No, it does *not* mean that. First of all, whether or not a council is "doctrinal" or "pastoral" or "disciplinary" is not what makes its decrees binding on the faithful. As we have seen, it all comes down to a question of authority. Ecumenical councils—all the bishops of the world teaching in union with the pope—have the highest authority.

Additionally, the Second Vatican Council did indeed address questions of faith and morals. While it may not have promulgated any new definitions of dogmas or responded directly to doctrinal questions of the day, the council still repeated teaching that had been infallibly taught.

In an audience on January 12, 1966, Pope Saint Paul VI said: "Given the council's pastoral character, it avoided pronouncing, in an extraordinary manner, dogmas endowed with the note of infallibility." He continued, "But [the council] has invested its teachings with the authority of the supreme ordinary magisterium, which ordinary magisterium is so obviously authentic that it must be accepted with docility and sincerity by all the faithful, according to the mind of the council as expressed in the nature and aims of the individual documents."

To put it another way: the question we ask ourselves should not be "What is the bare minimum I am required to adhere to as a Catholic?" The bishops, meeting in an ecumenical council and teaching together in union with the pope—even when "just" teaching on non-doctrinal matters—are still shepherding the Catholic faithful. A conscientious Catholic may disagree with assertions regarding non-doctrinal matters, but even still such teachings should not be uncritically dismissed out of hand.

94. Are the decisions of a pastoral council infallible?

The nature of a council—pastoral or doctrinal—is a somewhat arbitrary distinction. An ecumenical council is an ecumenical council: regardless of what other modifiers or descriptors might be applied, an ecumenical council consists of the bishops of the world teaching in union with the pope.

When it comes to the protection of infallibility, the questions of *authority* we have discussed above are the operative questions. One also must consider what is being said: as we have seen, the question of infallibility is really a matter pertaining to propositions rather than whole documents. But we can say clearly that the bishops gathered in an ecumenical council in union with the pope teach authoritatively, and even if a proposition is not infallible, it must be accorded the respect due to the teachings of an ecumenical council.

95. Were any of the other councils this controversial? In other words, did any of the other councils also spawn offshoot groups who claim that the Church had clearly abandoned the faith based on what a given council said?

Because of the nature of ecumenical councils and the context in which they are convened, each and every council was controversial, and each and every council had groups who did not want to adhere to the council's teachings. Councils are called when there is some great need in the Church, typically in response to a prominent heretical teaching that is spreading and causing discord and erroneous belief throughout the Church. Human beings don't often take too kindly to correction; so when Rome spoke through the mouth of the council, in most cases those who were being corrected did *not* mend their ways and then openly dissented from the council's teachings in the aftermath.

Even a so-called "pastoral council" is not immune to this. The Second Vatican Council yielded a great deal of dissent in its wake. In fact, the dissent following this council is quite complicated to sift through, as it can be seen coming from two separate camps: those who claim to be implementing the council's directives through what they call the "spirit of Vatican II"; and those who disagree with what the council said (or what they interpret it to have said) and thus deny the validity of the council.

96. What if I don't like what a particular council says? Am I bound to follow its decrees?

Once again, this comes down to a question of authority. What exactly is the authority with which a council teaches? As we are focusing here on ecumenical councils, we have seen that such councils have supreme authority over the universal Church, both disciplinary and doctrinal. The council's authority lies in the office of bishops as the successors of the apostles, teaching together in union with the pope, the successor of Peter.

Moreover, we should be diligent and honest when assessing *why* we ask questions like this. We want to avoid an attitude that asks, "What is the least I can do and still call myself a faithful Catholic?" The question should not be "I know the council taught this, but do I *have to* adhere to it?" The purpose of any ecumenical council is to sanctify, to get souls to heaven. Whether the council is doctrinal, disciplinary, pastoral, or something else in nature, the council fathers have the salvation of your soul at heart. Trust the Holy Spirit.

Of course, I realize this is a practical question. For the sake of argument, thought experiments, or trying to draw lines around a council's authority, the question can be very helpful.

Finally, because the ecumenical councils are protected by the Holy Spirit from definitively teaching error in matters of faith and morals and operate under the teaching authority that Christ granted the Church through the ministry of the apostles and their successors—particularly when teaching together, in union with Peter and his successors—placing oneself above a council and disregarding its teachings is a dangerous thing to do. Certainly there is a distinction to be made between doctrinal and pastoral or disciplinary matters, but it is not appropriate to pick and choose among the decrees of the councils.

97. Are there councils that others claim to be ecumenical but that the Catholic Church does not recognize?

The Eastern Orthodox churches sometimes recognize as ecumenical the Quinisext Council (see question 98), the Fourth Council of Constantinople (A.D. 879–880) (not to be confused with the Fourth Council of Constantinople in 869–870, recognized by the Catholic Church), and the so-called Fifth Council of Constantinople (A.D. 1341–1351).

98. Quinisext Council—why do the Orthodox accept this as part of the Third Council of Constantinople, but Catholics don't accept it?

The Quinisext Council takes its name from the fact that it was intended to follow up on and complete the work of the fifth and sixth ecumenical councils (Second and Third Constantinople), and is also known as the Council in Trullo (a term that refers to the domed hall in Constantinople where all three of these councils met). The Second and Third Councils of Constantinople did not pass any disciplinary canons, which was seen as a deficiency and something that needed to be done in order to complete those councils' work.

In A.D. 692, around 215 bishops—all from the East —met in Constantinople and passed 102 canons. These canons affirmed the councils that came before, but mostly dealt with ritual practices, liturgical guidelines, morality for clerics and laity, and other such disciplinary matters. Emperor Justinian II attempted to use this council to create a common canon law that would be used throughout the Church, in both East and West, and the bishops present tried to impose certain Eastern traditions and practices onto the West, including married clergy. These canons were never accepted in the West, however. The Orthodox called this council ecumenical, but as it was never ratified by the pope, it is not recognized by the Catholic Church. In fact, Saint Bede the Venerable (d. 735) called the Quinisext Council a "reprobate synod".

99. Why does the Catholic Church not accept them?

In order for a council to be considered ecumenical, as we have seen, the pope must ratify its decrees as such. If another Christian ecclesial group identifies something as an ecumenical council but the pope has not ratified its decrees and declared it to be an ecumenical council, then it is not officially recognized as one by the Catholic Church. Of course, this does not mean that the decrees of such a council would necessarily be false or untrustworthy; simply that it was not an ecumenical council. For example: if a group of Anglican bishops were to gather together and declare solemnly that a valid Catholic Mass confects the Eucharist and that the doctrine of transubstantiation is true, they would be absolutely correct—but not through any teaching authority of their own, and certainly not through the authority of an ecumenical council.

100. Can I read certain council documents with a "critically obedient eye"?

This question is related to the question of each document's weight of authority and infallibility. Even those documents that infallibly and solemnly defined dogmas have certain *propositions* that are infallible, but the whole document is not necessarily infallible.

Many council documents express the opinion of the council fathers or their pastoral concern on a given matter; many of them give disciplinary directives or give instruction for practical changes in Church life; sometimes these documents suggest ways to bring the Church's teaching into the contemporary world. On these and many other points, it is certainly possible (even respectable) to read the document with a critical eye, discerning along with the Church. But we still must respect the authority of the council fathers.